T0343522

CONNECTION

THE EASIEST SOLUTION TO THE WORLD'S GREATEST PROBLEM

Rabbi Asher Gottesman

RISE
BOOKS

Cover design and illustrations by https://www.fiverr.com/alonda
Jacket and interior design by Neuwirth & Associates, Inc.

Library of Congress Cataloging-in-Publication Data
Available on request

ISBN 978-1-959524-08-3 (hardcover)
ISBN 978-1-959524-13-7 (eBook)

Printed in the United States of America
First Edition
10 9 8 7 6 5 4 3 2 1

This book is dedicated to my children and my children's children, to their children, and all children of the world. You have taught me as a parent that unlike former generations where they believed we as children must love our parents no matter what, I am blessed to know that my job, which I take with honor and pride, is to love YOU no matter what. Thank you for being my true family, community, and connection.

TABLE OF CONTENTS

Part Three: What You Say

Part Four: What You Embody

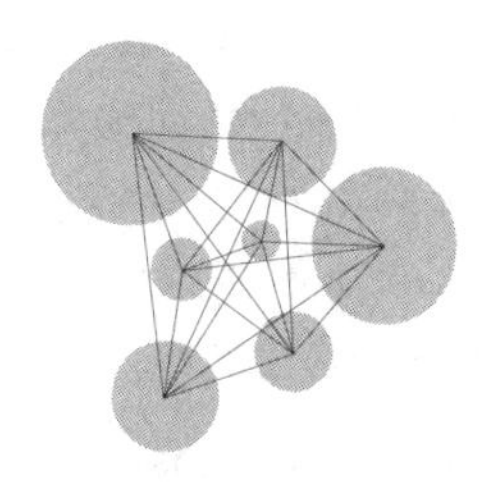

INTRODUCTION

Hey, I'm Asher. I've been to hell and back. I'm about to take you on a journey not because I expect you to care about my experience but because I'm interested in sharing what I've learned as an addict in recovery in case it's useful to you.

Do you remember building forts as a kid? Maybe you owned a set of plastic, flexible poles as I did, that when fastened together, worked to create a structure. Something that stood on its own that you could lie under, that reached upwards, that kept you safe. Something constructed with your own two hands, and so it was personalized, customized. It held a hundred potentials for what you could do with it, what it could be, and who you could be when standing underneath. Building this fort was as exciting as the games you could play once the assembly held firm because you had connected the parts, because each pole fed into the other in a way that made sense to you, that stood solid, and you understood your tent from the inside out.

This is how fun it can be for you to build connection. If you feel disconnected in the first place, you may experiment with thinking of a piece of you as loose or fallen off or even missing. Sometimes it's several pieces. Sometimes, the entire structure has collapsed.

Disconnection is an erosion that happens over time. Often, we don't realize it's happening until the house has crumbled. We look around and tell ourselves that something is wrong with us because we aren't like anybody else. Because we are homeless to ourselves. Maybe this belief began in your family system, with a gut–wrenching, soul–smothering feeling you were a stranger looking in, that you did not belong. Maybe disconnection reared its head in your life later, at school, with friends, as you tried to relate to other kids but could not find your people. That childhood doom you would never be picked for the team, find your group, or learn the secret handshake.

Whoever you are and whenever it happened, the lie the disconnected parts themselves hiss at us is that we're the only ones experiencing this pain. We're the only ones feeling alone. And it whispers our worst fear: *It will never change.*

Bullshit. Of course, it can change. The most important point of this book is that connection can be made again. It can be built. All it takes is your desire and dedication, and then it is already happening. Who cares how long it takes? It only matters that you're doing it.

Disconnection is not a permanent state, and those whispers are not written in stone. They are not God's voice, they are not facts. Those whispers are songs you've been singing without noticing that the key is off, that this is not your tune, that you can turn the noise off whenever you are ready and play something else. Even if the song has been echoing inside you for decades, blocking the light, obstructing the flow, tightening the darkness around you, nothing is wrong with your bones, with your spirit, with your poles. You can find your footing again. You can stand grounded with a house to hold you. You can begin to hear a melody.

You are doing so now with this book in your hand.

What do we do when we want to find connection again? How do we combat the cancer of loneliness, of something–is–wrong–with–me–ness, of disconnection? How do we right the ship of our inner world, feel whole again, and rebuild ourselves into our highest, best version?

That is what this book will cover. The how, given to you in small actionable increments, each one of them the path towards creating a big life filled with connection. Before we get into the how, before we dive in, please let me say this: how is not complicated. It is simple. And yet it is difficult because the how is constant, it is a practice, it is imperfect and messy, which requires grace and forgiveness, two of Disconnection's greatest enemies. That means Grace and Forgiveness haven't been allowed to stick around a lot before today, and now you suddenly want them to come over and live with you. It doesn't mean they can't move in, but it requires you to bear the discomfort of having their warm tenderness spread throughout your body and let it feel strange because you are doing something new by having them reside wherever you go from now on. Tolerate the way Grace and Forgiveness hum in the face of all the discordant loneliness you have been listening to because connecting again is supposed to jar you. Rest easy that jarring is the sign you are changing and shifting, no longer stuck in disconnection.

Nobody expected the life I lead today, least of all me. I fought for this life – I fought through not belonging, discontentment, addiction, losing people, selfishness, and self-hatred. I fought through supreme discomfort caused by supreme disconnection. Finding myself through recovery, in 12 Step rooms and beyond, was the beginning of my healing. I do not want to cheat you out of your journey, out of your fight, and yet, if I can make it even a little easier for you, a little smoother, or a little clearer due to what I have learned and seen, then the pain of my journey will have been more than worth it.

Though I am a Jewish man and a rabbi, though I am an addict in recovery, though both the 12 Steps and the Old Testament intersect throughout these pages because both are woven into me as a human, I'm a realist. I am both spiritual and secular. I am about human connection above religious dogma or rules that tell us how it must be done. Please trust me when I say this book is as much for those who are not Jewish, not assimilated with any faith, and not addicts as it is for those who are believers or in recovery. You do not have to be a 12 Step member for these words to benefit you. Actually, I'd like for you to consider this book as the place to turn if 12 Step meetings and houses of worship are the last spots you'd ever go. Because the beauty found in those rooms is distilled here precisely so you will not miss out on messages that can help your whole life simply because of the method of delivery. This book is for you, wherever you are and however you are, for the disconnected, isolated, or lonely, despite labels. Though I may use words like God or Higher Power or even almighty, please use your own word, please fill in the blank. Our DNA is wired to connect, and my intent is for this book to be an active supporter of you, you trying to better yourself, you showing up for you, using names that are right for you.

Welcome to where we come undone, and we overcome through forming a deeper relationship with ourselves and the world. In this book, we will discuss how to get to know yourself, how to get to know others in relation to yourself, how to find service, passion, and purpose, and how to put your new thoughts and beliefs into words and actions to create community. My wish is for you to apply these bite–sized morsels with ease, with patience, with dare I say fun, and to fall in love with your life. You deserve to love life, and love yourself in this life. You deserve to feel connected to who you were, who you are and who you are becoming. You deserve to feel connected to other people, to animals, to nature, and to whatever invisible force is keeping this whole thing going.

Because it's you. You are keeping this whole thing going. Each of us is that powerful, beautiful and needed to connect everything and everyone together.

Part One

WHAT YOU BELIEVE

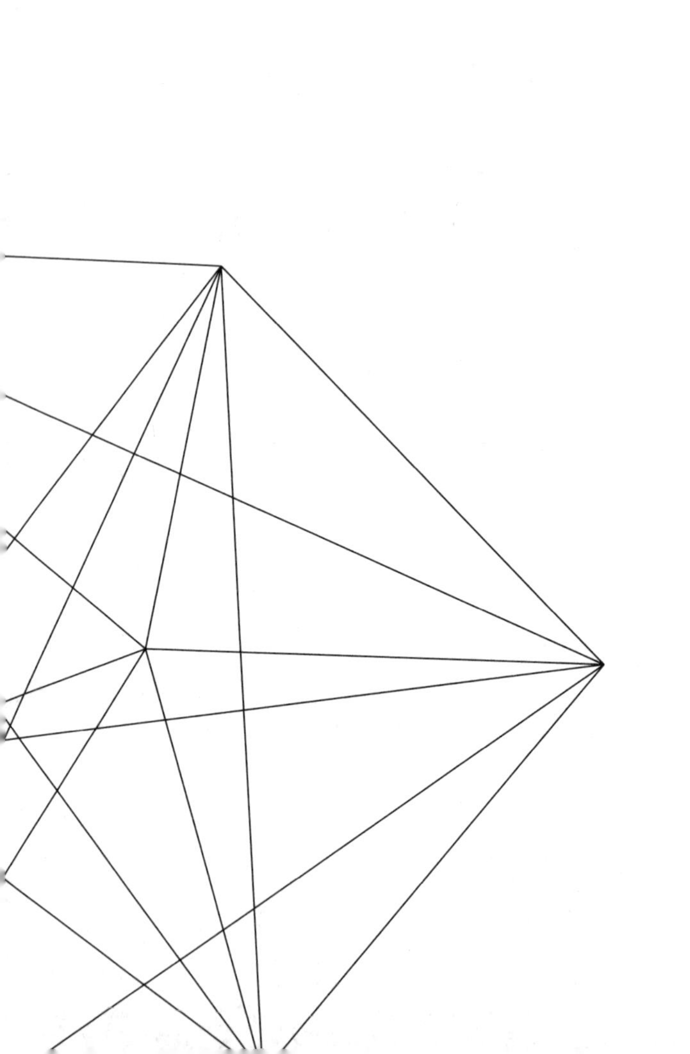

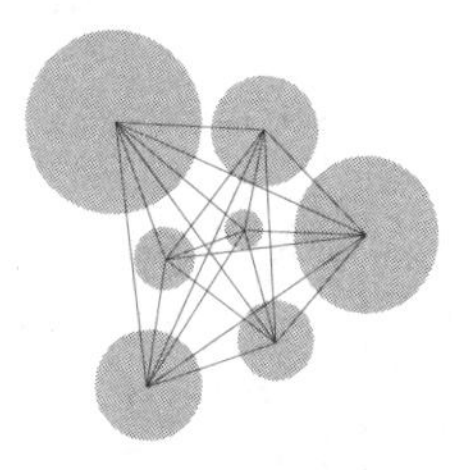

Conversation One: From Unloved to Loved

The first time I can remember feeling disconnected – a dropping sensation that thudded in my stomach – I did not know what it was. I was eight years old, and my parents had accepted a sabbatical in Israel so my father could further his studies. Shortly after our arrival, there was an emergency back in Los Angeles that my parents had to return to quickly. I stayed back in Israel with a newlywed couple, friends of my parents, but whom I hardly knew. I was separated from my parents, feeling as if I'd been separated from the box all my poles had come in and from the instruction manual, too. I remember knocking on the door of the couple, asking them if my parents had told them about my little problem, which was that I was deeply afraid to sleep by myself. Neither my mother nor my father had told them about my fears of the night, and in their confused, untested, somewhat exasperated response to me, I felt an immediate weirdness, an otherness, a belief about me settling in that something was wrong with me. I begged the couple to let me sleep on the floor of their bedroom just as I had begged my parents to sleep in their closet before they'd left for Israel. Luckily for me, they agreed. They let me. They allowed me the comfort of companionship during slumber.

But a feeling of unlovability had already begun to snake through my bloodstream. Every night, I tucked myself into shame – shame about my inability to sleep alone, shame about asking for what I needed, shame that my parents were gone and why did they leave me behind, how could they leave me behind, and what did that say about me? That I was worth leaving behind? That my nightly terror wasn't even something to prepare others to help me with? A child's perspective isn't necessarily the reality, but it is their reality, it is their pain just as my abandonment and loss was real for me, even if my parents were great parents in many ways. I fed my self-proclaimed unlovable nature with ice cream. The ice cream became like a medicine, intended to numb my nighttime discomfort. And it worked temporality, but it didn't work long enough or hard enough. The shame was so much syrupier, so much thicker, so endless, so strong.

Even after my parents returned from Israel, my sleep fears could not be mitigated, as if a Pandora's box had been let out too far for too long and had infected all of me. I faked sicknesses at my birthday slumber parties so my friends would have to leave, so I could go back to my parents' closet. I forced my friends' parents to walk me home from their homes whenever I tried to sleep at a friend's house. I just couldn't do it. I was the son of a prominent rabbi, and I couldn't sleep like a "normal kid." I could barely sleep at all, could barely rest, could barely stop my spinning, worrying mind.

Actually all I could do by that point was eat ice cream. The problem – that I felt unworthy of loving – had grown on its own, and oh, that poor boy. I see him still, I still feel him. The only difference now is that I love him.

I believed I was unlovable as I kid, and so I hid from the world. Later, the hiding morphed as I ducked behind money and ego, behind addiction and agendas and dazzling disguises like giving, so I didn't have to love because I didn't know what it was and didn't have any for myself to give to others. I always need more love from you, way more than I deserved if you were basing it on how I treated others in terms of depth and authenticity. I was so busy and shiny and distracted and scared that I showed no one myself because I didn't love that self. I couldn't know that self. I begged for love, searched everywhere for love, cheated for love, and was certain that love hated me, that the concept of love had turned against me.

It's no surprise I ended up empty–handed.

I know now that love does not have to be achieved. Love is something you simply are. There is no way to get it. The Universe cannot give you love because you are love. It doesn't need to be given to you, earned, or made. It is discovered. It's discovered through small movements inside oneself and repetitive healthy acts outside of oneself. As we take steps towards meaningful, humble, pure connection, we begin to thaw. We want to start putting down our phones, our cigarettes, our to–do lists, and to find our love, to be our love, the love we already consist of when we let everything else fall away. There is no such thing as unloved or unlovable once you know this. Love is connection. Connection is love.

Love is its own living thing. What you experience, reveal, learn, and become from love will be its own living thing. It requires doing nothing but being everything you are – imagine the effortlessness in that after all the hustle and trickery you have been using.

Love is contagious. You have to know this; you've seen this, right? You'll take your good feelings and use them to motivate yourself to do more for others without expectation, surprising even yourself, and suddenly, everybody around you does the same. You will tell yourself you are someone generous and kind and believe it because you will witness yourself actually doing it, and it will make others want to do it. You will see a stranger and talk to them. The stranger will pay it forward. You will drop groceries off in at–risk neighborhoods with nobody knowing it was you because you had the thought to do so, and then one day, somebody random will bring you flowers. It's an energy. It's about matching up. You will see your lovableness everywhere, reflected back to you constantly, projected everywhere once you know you are lovable.

You will be living your life as the love you had been seeking all those years. You will show yourself that you are not disowned and see in real–time how much love you deserve. Start by talking to the parts of yourself that crave connection the most desperately but are sure you'll never get it, the parts of you that felt the most unloved. The parts of you that you most want to blow up, bury alive, push away to Neptune. Bring them in. They need to be acknowledged and spoken to. They need to be loved! These are the parts that need your love the most! Ask those parts of you what they need, and listen to them. What hurts them? What do they believe? Give those parts alternative thoughts, offer them different perspectives, and be with them. Be with them. Their answers might change from one day to the next, and that's okay. It's responsive. It's fluid. It's intuitive. It changes daily. Keep asking. Keep listening to ALL OF YOU. Keep loving all of you. This is where your disconnection dies.

Yes, this work demands consistency, a constant checking in on ourselves but it's the most important thing you can do today, way more important than any goals. Because your wounded parts are calling the shots and won't let your life goals become actualized if you don't hear what they're begging for if you don't lead yourself into wholeness. Wholeness breeds connection. By better understanding our motivations and intentions behind the unloved parts, what we need and fear and feel, we move out of our heads and get into our hearts. Our heart space is unending. Our head space is tight and full of spirals.

We have to strive to be willing to let go of the habits and the armor of feeling unlovable and the identity that came with it. We let ourselves remember who we forgot we were; no matter what, we were born worthy and whole and lovable and always will be.

But we cannot give what we don't have. We have to strive to believe good, think good, and feel good. We have to strive to love ourselves enough to want to love ourselves more. We are more than lovable – we define the word.

You are part of the meaning of the word *love*.

Question for You

Let's begin by looking in the mirror. Looking into your own eyes. What do you see there that is lovable? Make a list, either by writing it down or reciting it to yourself out loud. Keep going, naming all the things you can come up with to love, whether it's physical features or the kindness you embody or the dimple on your cheek you have liked since you were five years old. Because that five–year–old is still inside of you, asking for your love. Love yourself as a practice, in black and white, out loud. Begin a lifelong routine to tell yourself, to think to yourself, to show yourself that this is true – your lovableness.

Nourish yourself by curiously observing without judgment as you search inside. Strengthening your compassion muscles is important; it provides a vantage point for learning to see similarities, overlaps, and understanding in other people, which only creates more connection. This comes from active participation.

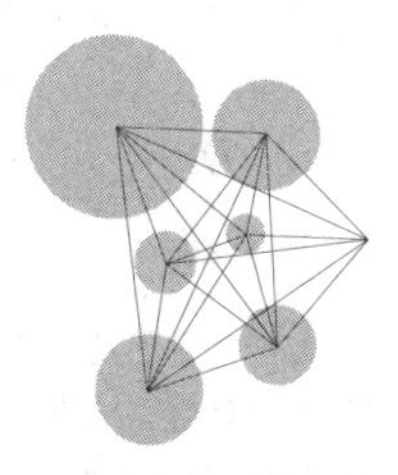

Conversation Two: From Victim to Victor

They say in the 12 Steps program you can't think yourself into the right action, but you can act yourself into right thinking. What that saying also refers to is acting from a place of authentic mercy for all parts of you, even the part that feels low, small, vulnerable, and scared. Instead of pushing that piece of you away, bring it into your fort. Give it time to speak. Hear it. Because the victim part of you is the part of you that leads your actions, leads your service, leads your victories. That piece of you will not stop, will not go away until you love it for its vulnerability. It wants to be protected. It wants to be safe. Don't be mad that part of you is there.

In this stage, we will identify and define the behaviors that disconnect us as well as the patterns, dynamics, and habits that keep us thinking we need to be losing so we will be loved. We need to overcome the parts of us that are over-focused on making others feel a certain way about us and instead tap into our feelings. We need to let go of how the victim role serves us, manipulates others to sympathize or pity us, give us attention and care. Whether consciously or unconsciously, we are asking to be rescued. This is the fight. To meet the needs of the victim inside of you and win. It is literally what makes you the victor. It is how you stop feeling helpless and hopeless, two of disconnection's favorite party favors.

There might be grief for becoming independent and self–sufficient, for being a victim comes with an attachment to what victimhood did for you. It is common to feel grief over changing who you are so you can become who you've always been, but it takes letting go and not knowing what will be. Victims need to know what will be. Victors face the unknown. Victims need to be saved. Victors are for connection.

Your addiction, aka your ego, will be your adversary. It tells you that love is need. It tells you that other people do not want you to be strong, capable, happy, rich, proud and receiving. It is fooling you! The people who are best for you, who are aligned with your highest good, do not see bragging as bragging, they see bragging as celebrating. The people who are best for you want you to widen your capacity to take in more – more money, more success, more wonder, more joy. Allowing this in for yourself and affiliating yourself with the people who support you is what makes you a warrior. Who is in your life that wants you to win and triumph?

Your messenger, your built-in reminder that you used to be a victim, and are now choosing to be a victor, will be the great discomfort you feel when you rejoice and proclaim what makes you shine. What makes you a star? What makes you light up? What makes you say, "Look at me!" You have nothing more to lose – you have lived disconnected. You can't go back to being alone. Whatever Power you believe in, who is grander than you, that Power wants you to dance about your life! To feel like a victor every moment, not because of what you have or earned or accomplished, but because of *who you are*: a person who loved the victim inside of themselves. Who took them in and fed them, sheltered them and said, "I got you, let's go have fun now."

You will flail and fall. You will feel conceited, selfish, and awkward. But the movement from ego back to Spirit, the shift from old patterns towards new conscious ways of being and thinking IS the whole deal, and it IS what makes you strong enough to be victorious. That IS how you build connection, one swing at a time, one thread, one opportunity at a time when you're at your highest vibration. You want the people in your life who are not chanting, "Beat him!" or "Be careful, don't upset anybody or take up too much room!" You want the people in your life chanting, "You already won!" Those who know it and hold you on their shoulders with glee.

So today – yes, today when you read this – we will do something scary. We will call somebody or send a text or write an email and tell somebody else to serve as our witness that we are proud of ourselves. And we will tell them why and what we are applauding. We will care less about their response and more about how we feel, which will hopefully be a gigantic leap in the air over who we are, how we lived today and that being ourselves is a victory all on its own.

You have to practice. You have to practice being seen as something other than a poor thing others have to take care of, should feel sorry for, should worry about. That is not connection. I promise. Connection is people raising their hands in ecstasy because you feel happiness, to feel happiness with you, including you to feeling it with them.

The Jewish response to victimhood is to take personal responsibility. That's not because we're so awesome; it's because, after so much experience with oppression, this was the only option we had not to waste our lives away. It was either accepting victimhood forever or taking some accountability to improve your life. This is how my ancestors withstood so I could stand here today. We didn't have the option to feel sorry for ourselves if we wanted to preserve, we had to want to triumph. The root of the word victim in Hebrew, *"yissurim,"* is the same as the one for self–improvement, which is,*"mussar."* The Talmud guides us to look inside if something has befallen them, not necessarily to feel justified for the pain or to consider that they deserve it, but to own it, own their part, improve, and move on. To use feeling as fodder to make us grow. We have been prey many times. We have been hunted on purpose for extermination. And so, we cannot, will not, be victims. The fact that there are still Jewish people thriving and surviving is proof that being victorious is a choice to make in terms of how we can look at ourselves and how we can ask others to look at us so we can live in connection to what is great about living.

Untether yourself from anybody and anything that keeps you in the victim story. Prove to yourself that is not you, they will see the charade crumble, they will see you come into who you are. But most importantly you will succeed at the only thing that matters, which is being the most you can be in this life. That is succeeding in your life. That is a connected individual.

You only get one life. Raise your hands and claim it, and connect with others who do the same. There is too much goodness all around you to ignore and to pull you down otherwise. Connect to the win that is life.

Question for You

We are not victims unless we decide to be, and if we do, my challenge for you is:

Tell me more. Tell me more about being a victim? When you ask someone else this question, can you hear the place where they are actually victors holding onto victim mentality?

Might it be that if you hear it in them, this dissonance, that it might also exist in you? Where might your victimhood be possibly reframed as you stepping into a victor?

I invite you to set the standard for yourself. Do it or don't do it, it's on you! Because we are all victors if we survive today, to this day, if we experience the privilege of getting older, of evolving, of feeling all the feelings. You are so much stronger, braver, and more spirited than that. You have sustained to this day. You have won. Connect with others in this – in this sharing of today. Connect with others by pumping them up and letting them pump you up. This is the best way to make sure connection is a joyful home you live under. This is the best way to ensure you will see tomorrow.

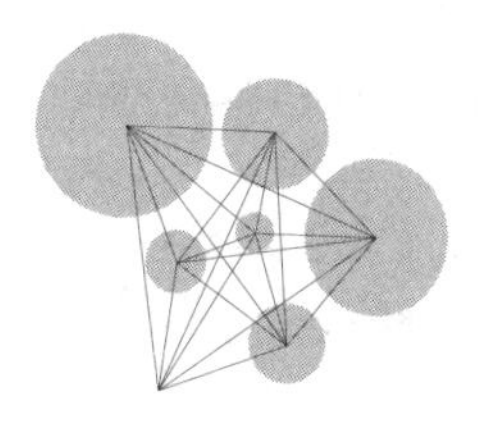

Conversation Three: From Knowing Everything to Curiosity

I don't recall a time when there has ever been more information available and so openly exchanged, so accessible. But there is a disconnect between knowledge and connection. Knowing only takes us so far. Connection is a full–body, whole–bodied experience.

If knowledge was enough, nobody would be lonely anymore. I love learning and believe knowledge has its rightful place in our lives! But it creates an addiction loop, its cycle of stuckness, because though knowledge seeking and finding, we keep seeking and finding knowing. And knowing won't get us across the finish line into loving and living freely because it's not a head–orientation. It's a heart one. Connection is a matter of the heart.

The heart is a curious space – it looks with wonder and acceptance, no judgment, and no binary answers. Seeing from the lens of the heart entails the ability to look from various points of view. From a heart outlook, everything can be a marvel, and everything includes the question: *how might I practice greater inquisitiveness*?

Because the heart does not crave black–and–white data, more information, or the illusion of shrewd wisdom. The heart expands, welcomes another perspective and still another, and because of how inclusive it is, it is the home for connection.

I constantly strive to make conscious efforts to listen to the dissenting opinion of others. I do this not because I'm so awesome but because it is unproductive to dismiss a person because of their views. I do this because I want to feel connected to others, to the world. Do it with me now, will you? Can you call to mind somebody you look down upon, downgrade, or downplay in your life as less knowledgeable than you? And can you begin by deciding in yourself to make a peaceful resolution to hear them and see them with curiosity to their valid beliefs? Can you accept them for just one minute, if not forever? Because I find that when people feel heard and allowed to be who they are, they are more likely to reciprocate the gesture and let you be who you are. If this isn't the building blocks of connection, I don't know what is.

Knowing can have a shut–down and shut–out tone to it. I am the master, I know it all, I have nothing to learn. The resentment and anger that follow this standpoint leads to much of the violence and aggression we see today. There will never come a time when we, as a whole human race, align on every single belief. We are a mosaic of cultures and perspectives, and no one takes precedence. There can come a time when we, as a whole human race, align in connection. And this will be possible only if we approach one another with curiosity, leading from the open land of the heart. This is how we bridge divides, but it requires us not to know everything. To not be the smart one, the educated, the master.

Curiosity births empathy. Empathy is connection's language. This does not mean absorption or deciding somebody else is the knowledgeable one now, but instead widening ourselves to match the infinite expanse of the heart where there is a breadth of potential and all of them count. Everyone counts. From here, we encourage expressions of love and decency, not uniformity but humanity.

This statement by Rabbi Levi Yitzchok tells me everything I need to know about the intention of my beliefs: "Don't worry about the state of someone else's soul and the needs of your body. Worry about the needs of someone else's body and the state of your own soul." I often ask why God has put so many challenges in the world and the only response I ever hear is for us to repair it. Judaism is a religion of protest. It's a religion where we don't know everything; we don't have all the answers, and we must deal with it, keep not knowing, keep searching with curiosity to make the challenges better, keep arguing and keep asking.

Curiosity asks open questions. Curiosity asks what, where, how, when, who, what if, and not necessarily why. Curiosity says tell me more about that. Curiosity does not give advice or make it about you. Curiosity reaches beyond our bubble of thought on purpose! Curiosity tolerates discomfort. Curiosity carries with the flexibility that knowledge does not. We come to the world, every one of us, with a unique gift we must offer, which makes up the jigsaw puzzle that makes the world perfect. If one piece is missing, the whole puzzle doesn't work. Curiosity lets each piece exist in its shape and size, and when each piece can, we have a connected section; we have a whole picture. The whole picture is the divine, which means we are all pieces of the almighty. By coming together in connection, we become God's partners.

Acceptance is the first key to many problems, but after acceptance and acknowledgment we can tap into the heart. From the heart, we can make life better for ourselves and others. God wants us to have everything. God wants us to make it happen for ourselves. God is curious with us. That's why we get to live life, and make choices, and learn, and love. Because God is curious and wants to see what we do and say, where we go, and where we grow. Living from curiosity connects us to God's spirit, to the piece of us that is a piece of God, and lets life be an adventure of the heart no matter what.

Question for You

Is there something new you can learn today with an open, curious mind and heart? Is there something you already know but can look at differently? Can you refute your stance by taking its counter argument? What other points of view are available to us if we simply employ an inquisitive nature and explore other perspectives?

At our probing and inquiring, we can recognize various narratives and options for the meanings we make, and we can learn. To expand. To blend into the horizon until there are no more lines. Feel the merging with not knowing, with wondering, and be free.

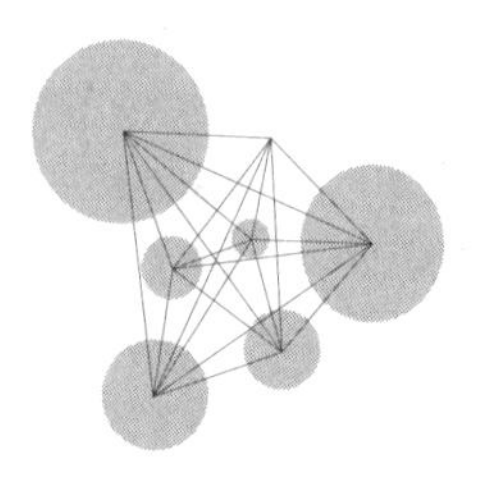

Conversation Four: From Lost to Vision

The opportunity for connection and purpose is all around us; important moments happen every day. It's just not every day we notice them.

I go to Israel every year to visit my father's gravesite on the day he passed. During this trip, I visited a drop–in community center called Zula that focuses on supporting young people. The youth there are primarily from very religious homes. Many have been rejected by their hyper–religious families. They've experienced and survived terrible traumas. Many are now battling addiction. Society has deemed them "at–risk," and the lack of unconditional love and community has indeed put them at risk at a great disadvantage. Still, they are beautiful souls and deserve to be safe, loved, and to feel connected.

They may feel lost, these "trouble youth," but vision is possible for them. The last time I was at Zula, my dear friend Avi told me there was a girl who suffered something horrific. This experience shattered both her sense of safety and connection. Avi would never share the girl's name, and I would never ask. But the story stuck with me, so I closed my eyes and asked God to please introduce me to this girl if I was meant to help her in some way.

As I was leaving, Avi asked me if I would light the Chanukah candles. As I approached the candelabra, a girl came over to me and asked if I would silently say a special prayer for her while I lit the candles. I asked her if she wanted to light them, to which she said, "No, just please have me in mind." During my prayer, something compelled me to connect with this girl. I gave her my information and let her know to reach out if she needed any support. We conversed for a few more minutes, and as I'm sure you've guessed by now, I later found out this was the girl from Avi's story.

I don't know in what capacity we will be in each other's lives. I don't know why. I only know we are not lost, not ever, if we are willing to open our eyes and see with vision. Ask for vision. And then step into that vision. I cannot be certain that we will ever cross paths again, me and this girl, but I am certain that when I was willing to connect in vision with someone who was lost – as lost as I once was – the universe conspired to make that happen. Vision is nothing more than listening to one's soul, to a higher consciousness. Our soul always wants the opportunity to be of service to someone in need.

The power of prayer and manifestation is real, and it is the warrior's tool of connection when we feel lost. We can set intention, a desire to do anything, and ask God to listen and nudge us to meet our goal through the vision He sees fit. To move us from feeling adrift. It may not be immediate. It may not be yet. But the vision always comes. Sometimes, we need to allow it time and reflection, and then the vision comes. Sometimes, we need to let gratification be delayed for the lost feeling to be there, to exist, and share its messages with us, too. Then, the vision falls upon us and leads us to connection.

We can live our entire lives from one vision to another, if we are open to it. For this exercise, I'd love to ask you to feel into a vision for yourself. Your ideal self. To imagine what a vision would look like fully or partially realized. Then, take the brave step of committing to the small and big actions each day that support them, trusting in your power of prayer, in your power of intention, and your power of manifestation because your vision is guided by something much bigger than you. Let that power drive you forward.

In the Bible, ensuring a sense of safety and community for self and others is a vision we are supposed to live by. I don't love that phrase *"supposed to."* So let's say we are destined to. Let's say it can be a vision we want to live by. Doesn't that vision sound like connection, like we can never be lost? I am not here to push religion on anybody, but I want to make it relatable, to show you the beauty, the fun, and the exciting part of faith.

I want to tell you a story of a rabbi who saw some of his congregants throwing stones at cars driving by on the Shabbos and "desecrating the holy day" as they drove by. (On Shabbos, the observant do not drive.) The Rabbi got up and yelled at his congregants, “How dare you meet desecration with desecration— these are God’s children just the way you are! If you want them to see your point of view, invite them to a Shabbat meal and show them the beauty within the home!” We will never be found if we meet lostness with more lostness. We cannot bring more lost behavior to existing lost behavior. We must strive to rise above. This requires leadership, an important part to carrying out vision.

For me, spirituality leads to my vision. It is the gateway to seeing my way back onto the map. For my brothers and sisters who are agnostic or atheist, you too have access to a source of guidance, although you are tasked with discovering what and who and how that goes. And though I don’t always envy your struggle (I have someone to blame and put my faith in), I admire your courage to wade into uncharted territory so you can find for yourself how to stay afloat. In the words of King David, even if a knife is pointed at our neck, it’s not too late for God to intervene and save us. And if it is not God–God, then I wish for you something else that you can say yes to, like love or hope or nature or music. So, it doesn’t have to be religious or godlike, but something that can guide us and protect us can help us find community, meaning, and a sense of safety. How do we believe while living and embracing the ethos of our practicality? For the agnostics out there, I don’t have answers, but I believe in you that you can do it. It is not my path to travel, but I am here with you. Focus on leading with whatever is good in us. Because without connection to ourselves, others, and something more, we don’t exist.

Faith is probably the greatest tool in my tool chest to combat the challenges I face in my life. The power of faith never stops amazing me, yet it can be a difficult muscle to exercise in the face of adversity and logic. Remember that not believing in anything is still believing. You get to choose. You get to trust in a job on earth for you. Doctors have told me that one's attitude does affect recovery and wellness. If I believe I will overcome– if I have faith, then I am more likely to have a successful outcome.

I find that when faith is most important, it's when I must dig deepest into my soul and believe that somehow, some way, I am not seeing the entire picture, but a force greater than me does, and it will ultimately be beneficial for me. What I find is that when others tell me it will be okay, or others tell me to have faith, I get angry, and I say to myself and sometimes to them, "Who are you to tell me it will be okay? Are you trying to make yourself feel better or me? Furthermore, who are you to tell me to have faith– do you have any idea what I'm going through?" So, I want you to know I understand, and I am with you.

I also find that it is most helpful when my friends tell me they are there for me, that they are walking with me and holding my hand, and that they are offering me a shoulder to cry on and remind me I can muster up the faith to believe it will all be okay for myself. Becoming unlost is a personal process. It happens inside when we are willing, seeing, when seeing someone else seeing with us, in whatever way that looks right to you.

Question for You

How might you exercise faith so you won't be lost, so when the outcome is seemingly negative, you can keep a smile on your face and walk towards your vision for yourself? How can you hold yourself so you do not have to fall into total misplacement when things get hard or don't go the way we want them to?

Write some of these answers down for yourself. Keep asking and iterating, create your survival kit and you will never leave yourself behind. When you are in the woods, deep in the forest of confusion, this can help you find your way out alive. Be your own flashlight, be your own right path.

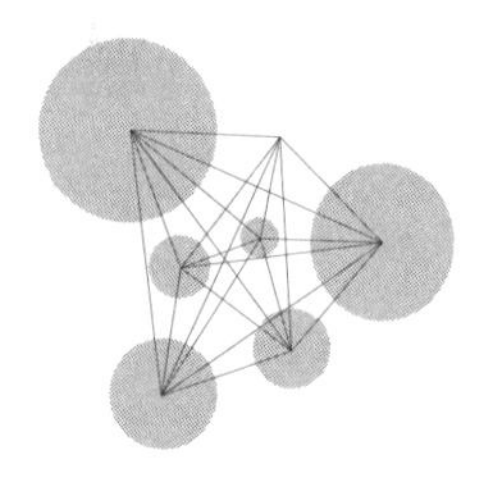

Conversation Five: From Rigidity to Flexibility

Being the baby in my family by a long shot, many years younger than my siblings, I always felt estranged from my brothers and sisters. I had nobody to talk to about this, no one to divulge my secrets to, no honest support. I felt separated, I felt like an unwelcome surprise, I felt squashed down. My older brother was my teacher at my school, and we didn't get along. When I was in the sixth grade, my dad was the head of that same school, and his solution to this issue was to move me to a different school so that my brother could stay and remain a teacher with him. What that meant was that I was worth less than my brother, that I didn't matter to my father, and that time with me wasn't a priority. An idea began to set in, take hold, and rot me from the inside: *I was the son of a rabbi, and this is who I was? Less worthy? Unimportant? Nobody.*

I felt insufficient. I felt not enough. It is my opinion that parents mess up their children the best way they know how. As a father myself now, I do not believe this happens through our mistakes as parents rather through not letting our kids have their own experiences and not listening to them without getting defensive when they share these experiences with us (even if we have provided everything for them.) The ultimate source of disconnection is denying a child their pain, which we as parents have no control over. All we can say – all we have the power to say – is, "I am so sorry. I made this decision because of XYZ, and I understand how you experienced it as painful. Please let me know how I can make it up to you."

According to psychologists, abandonment trauma is a fear–based response that stems from experiences of felt abandonment, whether that be from the death of somebody significant, the breakup of a family unit, or childhood neglect from primary figures who were physically or emotionally unavailable. I suppose I had this. I suppose I still do. I also suppose that its cure, or its healing, or the way I could have moved through that trauma as a child would have been to have been heard. To have been given the space to express this feeling of abandonment and for it to have been acknowledged as my real experience, whether it was my parents' experience or not.

To be compassionate, a good listener, patient and empathic, to teach the elements of connection, which are never the elements of a fixed game, is to accept that people understand things differently than we share them. My parents gave me everything, but I felt I was not connected to the family. I felt disposable, like a remainder in a math problem, like an unnecessary part. It didn't feel good, and it created so much pressure, this idea that I was the unwanted one and that it was my fault that I was unwanted in the first place for a reason I desperately tried to figure out. This position in my family felt so firm, so fixed. And so the idea felt so firm, so fixed that I was unworthy. The combined weight of my own unrealized internal expectations and rigid interpretations was a blanket too heavy for the plastic poles that were supposed to hold up my fort. Worst of all, I believed I had nobody to talk to about it.

The analyses we make seem logical to us when we make them, especially as kids. These meanings twist and turn and stack on top of one another into a coiling belief system based on the beliefs we've previously constructed about ourselves. That is to say, we don't see other options, other meanings, other than the ones that make sense with the ones that came before it, unless we learn how to be flexible in our thinking. So, if you have bad thoughts about yourself at a foundational level, the thoughts to follow are most likely to be disparaging ones, at last until you learn how to choose your thoughts or that you are more than your thoughts through the help of a tool like meditation. How to take one set of facts and the feelings we experience due to those facts and consider there are many points of views, perspectives and directions we can take about what it *means* in relation to our lives and ourselves – that is a skill necessary for connection.

If we have rigid, inflexible narratives and struggle to see the mountain from all its sides, to walk around the mountain and see what it looks like from another view, then we have no way of connecting with others who see something else or with flexible minds. If this is you, please consider killing the rigid meanings, beliefs, and old stories you've held. Yes, destroy them instead of yourself.

You stop the stories created by your childhood or your family by creating your own now as an adult, by admitting that you have been lonely and lost in service to those negative stories, and now can move forward with full intention and willingness to be found by the new meanings you choose, you write. Because those old stories about you were never true. We picked them before we knew what we know now, before we knew we had the freedom to choose otherwise, before we knew we were being influenced before we understood thinking for what it is before we can think for ourselves.

Even though we didn't pick our beliefs consciously as children, we now have a choice. And by not changing our rigid beliefs, we are still choosing. During childhood, we did not know. We were not guided. But that is why we're here, covering it in this book, as it is an essential rung in the ladder of connection. Because it is never too late to realize we can land on different interpretations. The facts and feelings are legit; that happened, you feel that way, and yet, it doesn't have to reflect poorly on you, about you, or further a tear up your insides. Your flexible thinking will let you connect to more people – those with different ideas and those with different ideas *about you*.

I made meaning of the events regarding my father and brother. This was my perception of Dad, and they weren't harmless assumptions either. They shaped how I felt, which can mostly be described in one word: alone. That aloneness grew to be the tallest tower in my landscape. When we are unyielding to consider other ideas and points of view, when I was dead set on proving my aloneness, then we have no other option but to feel unworthy; if we are not willing to relinquish the lonely feeling we may have become used to, we are deciding to commit unbendingly to loneliness and disconnection. Let's not do this. There are other pathways. There are other ways to feel. Turn that tower into something beautiful. Or at least less painful. One day you will see that that is beautiful.

Trust me, I know what it's like to take the bleak path and ignore all the joyous puddles glimmering with gratitude. Countless pools of hope invited me to cool off and swim in joy, and I ignored them until I thought they had eroded and disappeared forever. Because they challenged my story and rigid sense of aloneness, of unworthiness, and every time I passed them over, I practiced believing I was dried up, that any glow had been snuffed out of me, that I was the type of child who deserved being moved to another school and sent away so that my father could side with my brother. Nobody told me otherwise. It sucks. And at some point, I had to tell me otherwise.

For a long time, I didn't believe it was possible to be anyone other than who *I believed* my father saw me as. I held an allegiance to it, a rigidity around it, as if it was factually who I was. And I let it color every experience, seep into the background of every relationship, I let it take over. I rejected anybody who saw me as anything else, anything more. What I believed was his view of me was the wallpaper of my world, and I had no idea I could take it down.

You can take it down. You can teach your mind to be as flexible about the meanings it makes of events and emotions as it has been inflexible to the one you latched onto. Unlatching is not so hard. It requires you to question, to be curious, to get off of your chair and walk around the entire mountain until you see all the vantage points. Doing this requires a willingness to change the story you tell yourself. Doing this requires a willingness to hold new beliefs. Doing this requires getting up out of the chair and moving. Doing this requires dismantling an old belief system and rebuilding new thoughts and new feelings, like updating your phone's settings. We upgrade our technology all the time, don't we? Why don't we update our thinking and choose a default setting of flexibility?

Realize you are sacrificing rigid beliefs that meant something to you that carried weight. This is real inner work. This is the beginning of changing our attitude and outlook. Allow yourself to stretch and stretch wider. I'm here to spot you.

Question for You

The word sacrifice in Hebrew literally means "to bring close, to bring forward." So now, together, we will close our eyes, bring our rigidity towards us, closer, even closer, and we will be flexible in terms of how we see it. That's right. Let's look at rigidity itself from more angles. How is it helpful? How is it serving us? How is it hurting us?

Please grab a pen and paper. Write down, "Dear My Rigidity," and for ten minutes, without editing, without letting the pen off the paper or the keys off the keyboard, I'd like you to make amends to your rigid wiring. How else could you look at Rigidity? As much as you dislike it or want to push it from you, as much as you deny it, I'm asking you to tune into where you feel tension, tightness, and resistance because that is your rigidity, and it wants your tenderness. It is a part of you. Thank it, ask to use its energy in new ways, invite it to morph. In short, be flexible about how you see rigidity!

After that, I'd like for you to take one event in your life that causes that same tense, tight, resistant feeling to crop up. Write it down, and write down how it made you feel. That event, your feelings, acknowledge them; let's not try to pretend them into something else. Can you identify the meaning you made about that circumstance, those feelings? And then, can you discover six, eight, ten other meanings that are possible? What other beliefs might show up, and what other stories are available? All are equally true and untrue, none can be proven, for they are meanings, they are outlooks. So you get to choose the one that works best for you and your life! Go on. Choose. Once you land on something you like, or like for right now, you can practice it, internalize it, you can even change your mind about it – you are practicing flexibility.

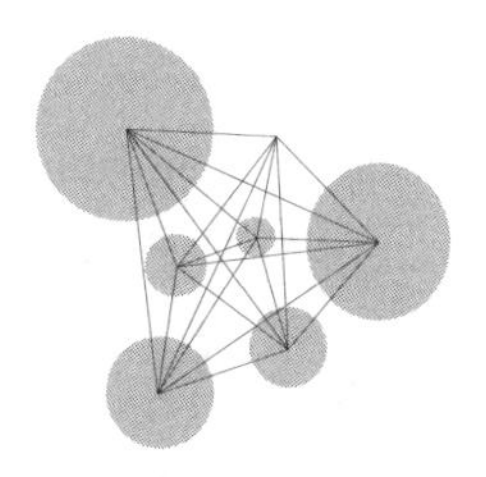

Conversation Six: From Self–Led to Guided

There is a big push for us to be self–guided, self–taught, self–motivated and self–self–self. But I will make a case against it as it pertains to connection. It's fantastic to be independent and resourceful and to know how to be disciplined with your efforts. We need to need each other too. And we need to need the make the space within ourselves in order to be guided, led by a power greater than us, led by others, led by the magical essence that comes from being part of a team. Everybody has gifts, insights and directions, and some can be good for us. It is only when we let go of trying to do everything ourselves that we can make room for divine intervention to come as inspiration. Inspiration is guidance from above. It carries the scent of connection, if connection were a perfume.

A question that arises is: how do we go from self–led to guided and still hold ourselves accountable? The answer is we surrender. We surrender to standing strong and tall in what we know. We surrender to humbly asking for help in what we don't know. We surrender to showing up every morning and saying, *Where will you have me go? What will you have me do, say, be?* And when we ask with full certainty that the path will illuminate, the clarity comes.

Inevitably, we will retake matters into our own hands. We're human. We will practice self–pity. Lose our temper. Think we know it all. If we seek connection, seek to feel connection within ourselves and outside of ourselves, then we cannot shame ourselves for it, for our humanness. The shame and guilt only perpetuate the behavior and keep self–seeking behaviors going. So, how do we motivate ourselves without shame? How do we get back on the proverbial bandwagon? How do we pick ourselves back up so we can drop ourselves into the easy flow of surrender once more and believe in the guidance that meets us from others and from our Higher Power when we simply ask for it?

We all have our strategies for this. So I invite you to take this time now, pause the book and write down what works for you. What helps you return to asking for help, to humility, to connection. Because when we only rely on ourselves and think only we can do all the things, there is little to no space for anybody else – whether a human, animal or celestial being – to come in.

Selfishness and self-seeking slips away the more we search for, nurture, and appreciate connection. I was having a conversation with a friend, and he said to me, "If I were an inventor, what percentage of invention would I need to see to fruition in order to be considered the best inventor of all time?"

And I replied, "Zero. Because the best inventors create for the sake of creation." Sure, there have been extraordinary inventions that have changed people's lives. Every invention leads to the next and the next, like a giant relay race, so one great thing cannot exist without all the great things that have come before it. That is to say, all the failed inventions led to the light bulb, to the printing press, to cars and airplanes. All the bulbs and presses and cars and planes that did not work allowed for the ones that did.

This means there is no I. There is only We. This means there is no failure and no "best." In a WE mindset, everybody is part of the win. Every inventor who worked on lights and electricity had a hand in the invention of the lightbulb. We can't control how everything goes and who goes with it, in what order. We can let go and let ourselves be guided, let each of us be our best self and trust we are part of the Great Things. What connects us more than anything is not the winning, but personally fulfilling meeting our individual potential, one inventor at a time, one creation at a time, one person at a time.

My point here is not to encourage you to fail but to give yourself permission to fail. To celebrate failure as a way towards success. To treat every no as another step closer to the yes. When failure happens, I want to encourage you to look at it as a lesson, a guide, and a message. Even if it leads to somebody else taking an idea to the finish line, the success has been achieved! It's not all about you. And it's also not without you.

Albert Einstein spoke about the "pursuit of knowledge for its own sake, an almost fanatical love of justice, and the desire for personal independence." I read this quote and feel lucky to be part of a culture that teaches me to wrestle, even with God. If your Source is the most important relationship in your life, you must argue with Source. You have to be real to Him, and you have to be honest and known to one another. So when you seek and receive guidance, it won't always be daisies. Sometimes, it will be fights and daisies. Somehow, though, someway, the Universe always ends up being right and getting my back.

Abraham was the first monotheist. He argued with God to save the city of Sodom from destruction. On first look, this may seem blasphemous. However, the almighty let Abraham know, so it goes, that humans are supposed to defend one another and remember that life isn't a zero–sum game. That we are all part of one, big, same family. I like this visual of a power greater than me, the power that can welcome disagreements and who loves what His creations have to say in response. Faith instructs us to love for free, and it tells us that when guided by a sense of unification, we are unstoppable. When we are self–seeking, selfish, and self–centered, we cause ultimate destruction.

In the 12 Step rooms, they say God is everything, or God is nothing. In my life, the truth is I have picked and chosen when I have faith and when I do not. On bad days, I pray for God's will for me, for wealth, success, and recognition, even though deep down, I'm aware that they won't ultimately make a difference in terms of how I *feel*. On good days, I pray for health and wellbeing so I can be a better man, a better father, and be guided to be the best human I can be, of the greatest service I can be to this world. On my best days, I pray to have the courage and strength to show up and carry out God's will for me with grace. Nothing more. To be led. Real faith is that whatever the almighty does is for the best, especially when we do not understand God's ways.

I cannot and do not judge myself or anyone else for not achieving this lofty goal every day without doubt or will creeping back in. Yet when I surrender and stay out of the results, when I pray that whatever is best for mankind happens and I mean it, I feel a life of truth align in me and I turn on like railroad cars in San Francisco.

There is much conversation about the collective anxiety of today's world and how children don't feel safe. What I believe when I hear this is that we lack connection, and connection can only happen from surrender, from the dropping away of ourselves so we may be directed. So we may trust the direction. If we all did that, we would have nothing to fight for or defend or worry about and everything to gain.

Question for You

How can you plug back into a power greater than yourself—whether that be a tree, a butterfly, whatever—so you can live a life of maximum connection? What can you control to create the outcomes you believe are best for your families, friends, neighbors, community and country? And what is not in your control – what do you need guidance for whether from other people or the Universe? Because Higher Power hasn't taken us this far to drop us. There are the things we can do and figure out for ourselves, and there are the things we can't do, things we need help with.

The greater you detach from results, the greater connected you will be in the world. We have no control. What we have is one another.

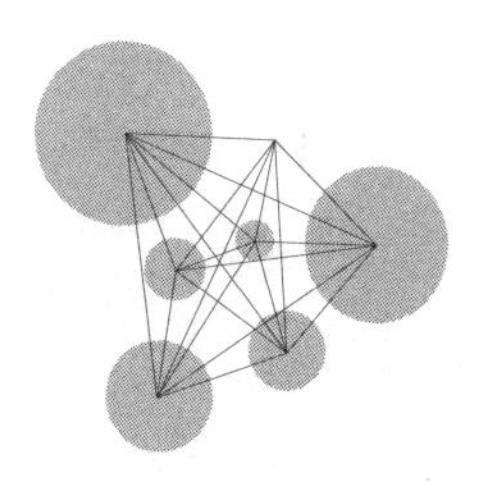

Conversation Seven: From Superiority to Equality

In a treatment center, everyone has a common goal, which is to improve, which requires supporting one another which requires accepting sameness. Equality. Oneness. It is the actual path to stop thinking only about ourselves, and oh, how freeing that can be. You get outside of yourself to come back into yourself. By focusing on the group, whether in therapy, because you live under a communal roof, or because of some shared unspoken unease, being together as one of many is the road we travel to connection.

Some of us spend our lives working hard to fill the gaps that ache, to decorate the spaces of emptiness so we don't have to feel them. Our lives become exhausting. We exist unknown to everybody around us as we hustle to try and belong, to try and prove ourselves, to try and achieve. Most of all, we exist unknown to ourselves. Perhaps the worst part of living in disconnection like this is that once we start the descent, it's hard to see we're even slipping; it's hard to stop the decline even when it becomes sharp and jagged, and we're covered in bruises and scratches because falling has a momentum to it. And it takes strength to stop the force of continual tumbling, especially when we live in a world that breeds this separation, that capitalizes and thrives on our cutting ourselves, telling us it's the way to earn the privilege of being on the planet.

No more. We don't have to earn our right to be here at all. We earned it because we came here. You are here. You have earned it; you have been picked. It's not a mistake. You are not a mistake. Neither is the person to your left or your right.

We don't have to struggle or suffer. It does not bring forth our worth or produce the love and care we seek from others. It does not create connection, not really, no matter how much people like to complain and moan to feel a semblance of closeness. It does not have to be hard, being alive. We don't have to do it the way everybody else does it. But – and this is the point – that does not mean your way is superior to someone else's. Their journey is as worthy as yours; neither of you is better nor worse.

We don't have to live sliding down, that is not the energy of life, that's not how it goes. Being close with others through whining and complaining isn't closeness, it's competition. Nothing is against you. That does not have to be the direction you go or the mantra you chant, decline is not the point of gravity. Gravity is holding you in place, grounding you, not pulling you down. Life has its hand gently on your back, it isn't shoving you. The only thing you have to do to feel that is decide to believe it. And when you do, you will see this is the case for every single body because every single body is equal, connected, one. The true definition of humility is I am no greater than or less than anyone else.

The lies are tempting. There is social media giving us a false sense of reality, creating anxiety by the millions, only showing us one side of life and insisting that if ours isn't like theirs we are less than, inferior, or better than and superior. There is a lack of interpersonal relationships that a pandemic has only eroded quicker and further than ever before. There is no communion, the absence of lifting ourselves in unison, the absence of honoring shared commonalities *in person* that offers an immense sense of safety, security, equality, and connection. It is rooted in the same in–the–roomness that used to happen in a place of worship, or concerts, or during live theater. The pandemic took more of our communal spaces. The more online we get, the scarcer those shared spaces become.

The 1960s may have given us the chance to question religion, becoming the first generation to break away from God, but what it did not give us is a replacement, an alternative anchor that works once we step away from our churches and synagogues and mosques to remind us daily – for it takes a consistent reminding – that we are equals. This period was unified in what people did not like as opposed to what they did like, they focused on the problem instead of a possible solution. People wanted peace and the end of war, yet did not offer a plan on how to get there. Getting there is it! Getting there is oneness!

Where is centrality, where is community, where is the realest reality central to being on Earth, which is that it's a miracle each of us is here? We are all miracles. That means we are one race, one faith, one people, one of the miracles. It's who we are, it's not an accident you are here. God gave you that breath, and wants you to connect mind, body, and soul to believing in the miracle of being a member of the Miracle family.

It must be in you. Impartiality leads to pure community and pure community is the mothership of connection. It must start in you, be of you. Yes, you, unique, individual, one of a kind you, who is as special as everybody else. You, connected, standing, reaching a hand out to another, knowing when two hands come together, that between your skin and theirs is the energy that made both of you. You can't measure energies as better or worse. They just are.

We move from superiority to equality by slowing down, even if it is antithetical to the pace our current reality promotes. Even if everyone in your family, your friends, your world moves fast, slow down so you can listen. Listen to yourself. Listen to your behaviors. Listen to nature. Listen to your Higher Self. Go outside, go somewhere new, and listen. The far too–overlooked act of connecting and becoming one of many begins with listening.

We find our sameness to others when we listen to our gut feelings, the inner voice that guides us, and then we just show up. And then that inner voice confirms that we have arrived. It's part of our connection process, to play and question and keep seeking until we find a yellow flag that waves at us to stop here. We deserve to decide who we spend our time with; we deserve to be with those who reflect back to us a life we wish to live and aim to live. We also get to push our edge and show ourselves what we're made of when we're ready for it, and we get to be honest with ourselves along the way.

It is not a mystery. It is not for the lucky. It is not too hard. It is not inconvenient. It will not happen instantly by tomorrow. It is not total crap. It is not trivial or stupid. It is not impossible because of your schedule. Those are all excuses to avoid what connection actually is.

It is humility.

When you connect as one of many, you see yourself as no different than anybody else, you see yourself in others and others in you. This lets you understand that connection is the reason we came here. Not to earn, not to one up, but to land in the room with others.

It cannot happen behind a screen, numbed out, or avoiding our emotions. Be still. And listen for the connection habits you can begin to assemble, listen to the wisdom of where you are unsure. Know yourself, push yourself, connect yourself. As you replace maladaptive behaviors, which drove disconnection, with harmonious practices that sink you into the comfort you most desire to live as yourself, you will find others living as themselves, too. Then everybody can be who they are.

In this place of one field, one plane, one family, we are never alone.

Question for You

Make some tea. Get quiet. Take out a pen and paper and begin planning. Give yourself time to explore and write down all your interests and passions so they can become openings, points of me–too between you and other people. Until we actively look for how we are not better or worse but the same, we can't access our full potential of love. So where can you lean into equality today, my valuable friend? Where can you meet people with interests and passions that overlap and synch up with yours? Start with this most obvious place – those like you.

Listen and determine where your community might be. It's right there, a place to start, to go, to find a circle that you can sit in. Then, make another list. A list of where you can go to feel most challenged, the circles you'd least want to sit in and identify those. And get ready to eventually change your mind by showing up and being proven wrong with those you thought were not like you.

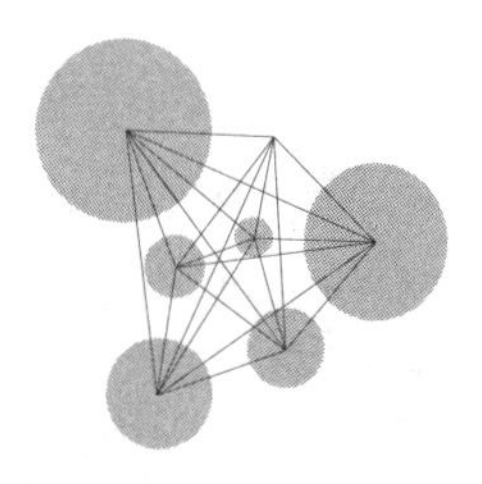

Conversation Eight: From Confusion to Service

Maybe you feel confused and aimless or frozen and buried under the rubble of uncertainty. It may be your self–esteem that needs building or your sense of self that needs discovering. Action is the seed that bears the fruit of the answers you are waiting for. Your answers, your fruit, not somebody else's. Taking action can begin through stillness, oddly enough, because stillness and self–esteem grow in tandem, organically, and give way to the revelation of what you want to DO, something you can do to give back. So you get quiet and still, and you listen inside, and you identify where you would like to show up and be of service. Where you can volunteer. Because doing is connecting, and connecting is doing. If you lack connection, doing something born from connecting inside to connect outside will free you from the loneliness. It is the best way I have found to begin my life.

Let's talk about how to get the most out of giving back no matter where you do it so that you can receive the highest gifts, not another addiction known as codependency. We won't go there. Codependency may be the one condition that afflicts us all. We are wired to belong, to seek love, to want to be needed...but sometimes, that grows out of control. When our focus on controlling others outweighs our self–care, we have entered the realm of codependency. Having value is essential, being needed and wanted is understandable, but bypassing yourself to fulfill somebody else's life, worrying about others more than yourself, and manipulating to force others to behave to your liking are examples of a human tendency taken too far. Making sure our spirit of service does not bleed into codependency is a job that requires vigilance and honesty. We can't trade in disconnection for codependence. The point of this is wholeness, wellness, connection with self and with others. We are ushering in balance.

Let us form an idea of where we can go and begin to be of service, and dive into doing so by pinpointing the activities we wish to participate in that move us and allow us to contribute ourselves with vigor and enthusiasm. This new doing – the spirit of service – will need space. Will need time. Will need energy. Where will it all come from? The time, energy, space and life force you need to do the thing your soul has directed you to do will require you to put down the thing you "use." Whether that is multitasking or screens, wine or ice cream, negative self–talk or an overly–fixated goal you cannot let go of, I have seen time and time again that the soul wants the bad habit that breeds disconnection to be gone. Trust me, the soul wants you to do what it's asking for, which will bring you to feeling good and complete. The soul, once you listen to it, wants you to connect. The soul knows what keeps you apart and numb and believing the lies that isolation, depression, anxiety, and ego spew because the soul is wiser than any other part of you. The soul will naturally, on its own, offer your disconnected parts as a place to take energy from so you can be of service so you can act with plenty of energy. You have more than enough to give, and we need your gifts. This is your chance to channel your focus.

When you think about how you are disconnected and from whom and from what, when you think of where your life might be lacking, where you are hurting for change or what you pick up to "cope," those answers will direct you to the reservoir that you can drain to start doing. For example, if you love dogs, maybe volunteering to walk shelter pups would be enjoyable. Or if you have a green thumb, consider stopping by your local community garden to lend a helping hand. If cooking is your thing, maybe there's a soup kitchen that could use your skills or an underpass where you can drop off dozens of premade sandwiches. There is no shortage of ways to be involved, and no act of service is too small, even if it's taking the garbage bins out for your elderly neighbors on Fridays.

Service is a thousand seeds of connection planted in the most fertile soil. You don't need to pay attention to the addiction, the place you go away from yourself. You won't need to. By beginning to allow yourself to be excited about where you will spend your time, by focusing on the good things coming in and going out, the good things you are doing, a sense of clarity blooms inside of you, and you will naturally begin to chip away at the resources that used to keep your addiction alive, and these resources will naturally allot themselves to the bountiful acts of service, and the place you are being beckoned, where you volunteer and give and are appreciated, will lead to a shift that happens on its own inside of you. Pride is a feeling that swells and spreads and warms.

But as it grows, prepare for your addiction to get mad! To protest! To shout, Hey, that's my time, energy and space! As willingness emerges, trust that your "disease," your self–hate, your addiction, or however it manifests for you, will be doing pushups in the back room, as they say in the 12–Step program, because you are beginning to shift your life is a threat to that old you. Ego is a creature of habit and pain, designed to keep you surviving. You are connecting not surviving. There is no bear or cheetah chasing you. So you won't want to focus on the back room! You'll be too jazzed about the new front room you're creating even if it feels unknown because it will be fresh and full of possibilities and people excited to see you and whom you are also excited to see. You will be excited to see you.

It is good that disconnection is threatened. Disconnection is being weakened. Keep chasing the area you are interested in and focus there, not on the detox and what you used to do. Because you are being made anew, not randomly – you are being of service from a place of integrity. Whether it's small actions like taking a short walk by yourself each day to bigger assignments like committing to regular volunteer hours, we go in first to go out, and this translates into a tremendous sense of love for yourself. Now you are showing up. Wow! You are doing what you said you would do. You are somebody! You are touching your worth. And a tenderness for yourself will snowball because of it, no matter what anybody else might think. You are. You can. It's you with you. You with you connection allows for you with others connection. Doing for others is a balanced, right–sized way that brings you to see that you are actually connecting to yourself and to them.

So, we are assessing our interests and putting them into service. We are doing something. Please know you can change your mind at any time. The service need not be philanthropic if you don't want it to be. This isn't martyrdom. If you like basketball, you can coach or create a league. If you were close with your grandparents as a kid, you can go visit nursing homes once a month now as an adult. If you volunteer somewhere, anywhere, for even two weeks, watch how that changes your life. It's the most practical way to discover deep connection and find meaning. Nobody is meant to fill us up; we must strive to do it for ourselves. Volunteering is the shortcut. It's the quickest way to douse yourself in a full bucket of self–respect. It doesn't have to be where you give back forever, and it doesn't have to be every day or even every week. But doing with no agenda other than to generously serve will become the nucleus of the new you. The You, you.

Before jumping into the acts of service, before discovering purpose that lets us begin to feel whole, remind yourself that you are leaving your home as an equal. Even if you serve others, even if others have needs you have fulfilled, do not show up at a volunteer opportunity letting separateness fool you or thinking you are better or smarter. Struggling, focusing on the problem, and divisiveness are disguised inertia. They will keep you stagnant and confused about who you are. We need to focus on what we want more of, not to call in more of what causes us to suffer. We're done suffering. We show up to do, to act from our way into loving so we can get the most out of living. And because being of service involves no compensation, it is essential to highlight this: you must enjoy it. Appreciating it is the pay. You must feel inside you want to give here and dedicate your time here. Otherwise, the antidote can lead to more proof you are taken for granted, taken advantage of, and should be resentful. Back to codependency again.

The key differentiator is your internal barometer, the knowing voice that shows up before you show up. And if that voice rolls its eyes or groans, great news! You have data now, and it's time to find another place to shower with your gifts. Pivot. You are allowed to pivot. The best part is: YOU HEARD YOURSELF. That is the center of all connection. This makes connection a pulsing, breathing force you can spend time with and tend to.

Listen to where you feel like you want to use your talents and share your gifts. Others are dying to see them. You are dying to see them. When we dig deep, not just write checks, but actually show up and do something with our whole bodies, the sense of loneliness, disconnection, and unease dissipates drop by drop on its own. You can volunteer your way into feeling better, not by deciding to become a selfless, self-righteous saint but by aligning with what you care about and how you want to make a difference.

And then caring in real time.

And then making that difference one minute at a time.

This builds a sense of self. This closes the loop. This locates the missing pieces, the poles that have rolled away, that are hiding under the bed, that are buried under boxes in the closet, that are covered in dust. You will build yourself again through the actions that make you buildable.

Question for You

Start this moment. Put the book down. Open your computer, call a friend, and ask for a recommendation, drive around and find where you will begin showing up in your local community with nothing in it for you other than to offer benefit to others.

There are websites designed to make it easy for you to find opportunities, community spaces like your local animal shelters and veterans' organizations, hospitals and schools and care facilities with volunteer efforts waiting for you to walk through their door. Watch any feelings of turmoil, aimlessness and uselessness vanish in the breeze. Nothing makes us feel so full as when we empty ourselves out in service to others.

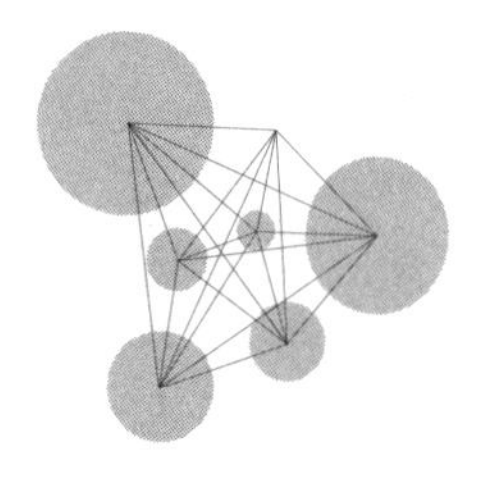

Conversation Nine: From Unhappy to Grateful

Gratitude is what leads to happiness. Fleeting happiness might come from external stuff, from shiny objects, but true happiness comes from connection. When you stop and realize the friendships you have, the challenges you have overcome, and the blessings you already have right now in this moment, joy is inevitable. So I want you to stop. STOP. Stop right now. Close your eyes. Imagine losing everything you have. Feel that. Feel it for a moment. Now, imagine getting it all back. How does *that* feel? That's gratitude. You can put the book down now. I'm sort of kidding, but not entirely, because I think that's the best thing I can teach you. If this is the only lesson you get out of the book—that you appreciate who you are and what you have today—I'll have truly succeeded.

When someone loses the ability to walk and learns how to walk again through hard work and perseverance, they experience a true sense of happiness about something so simple, something we all take for granted. Anything that we slow down enough and pause long enough to appreciate results in lasting joy. When we overlook our gifts, whether they be our abilities, connections, family, or health, we cut ourselves off from the connecting force that is gratitude.

Gratitude is not complacency. It lets us fulfill our potential in this world because it acknowledges what we already are and have at our disposal. One way to be grateful is to write a gratitude list daily, to commit to that small but mighty practice, and to hold yourself accountable by sending it to others. They might even send theirs to you if you invite them to.

Happiness is not a permanent state, but unhappiness can be. We have to strive to work for happiness because happiness comes from the work. From the striving. Few people want to be close to an unhappy person. It becomes a warning, a blinking sign, a repellant keeping others away. Gratitude is the antidote to this emotional response, and gratitude lets you see beyond the self. Gratitude is the warmest vibe in the world that ushers others towards it. Gratitude pushes us to believe in ourselves, in others, in who we can all become together. I remind myself that I am as gifted as every one of us, yet that doesn't make me special. It makes me responsible for appreciating my gifts, and for sharing my gifts, as they aren't mine; they are gifts from the Universe around us. It costs you nothing to look at the present moment and ask yourself what is already abundant, joyful, and right.

However, life happens, and it's hard to be thankful ALL the time. We will forget. We will fall. We will hurt. For this exercise, please think about when you aren't grateful and to plan ahead. To consider what movement you can make towards strengthening the gratitude muscle and at least bolstering yourself through whatever tough time you're going through by allowing yourself to feel and include happiness. And to let others rush towards you, leaning on the connection possible despite times when appreciation may be harder to come by. I have found that being honest about what is going on, what is wrong or bad or unfair can bring people together, not in the spirit of commiserating, but in the spirit of sharing. Of demystifying. Of me, too.

Camaraderie, when things are challenging is a beautiful thing. It is something to be grateful for. If you let yourself be grateful for it, it will bring you so much joy. That joy and connection in times of hardship, plus the chosen positive outlook to focus on what to be thankful for will combine into an elixir that will undoubtedly deliver you out of your tough times.

I know many families who have lost children.

The first question I ask myself is always: Why? I believe in God, yet I have no idea why God would ever allow for this pain and suffering to exist.

Then I ask myself: What can I learn from this to be a better parent and a better human to not let such a tragedy be in vain?

Lastly, I ask myself: What is there still to be grateful for? For me. For them. For all of us. Because I want to connect with them, and coming to them with my sad, horrified, sorry energy will not offer them anything else other than what they have. To come to this family with more, with sympathy, yes, and also with gratitude for what is left behind in the loss they bear, at the very least offers them a different light to bump up against or snuggle up to. I want them to feel me there for them to connect shall they wish to. Making myself available for connection might be possible only from a place of appreciation. Darkness is disconnecting, and negativity is too, and though it is necessary and important to bear witness, to hold space for feelings, especially the biggest and hardest ones, it is also necessary to remember that the living are still living. And to be grateful for the next heartbeat, the next breath.

I am reminded of a story where a therapist brought a husband and wife to a Rabbi, asking for help to resolve a conflict. The wife stated her case, to which the Rabbi responded, "I hear you, and you are right." The husband then stated his case, to which the Rabbi responded, "I hear you, and you are right." The therapist then said to the Rabbi, "How can both parties be right when they share opposing views?" to which the Rabbi responded, "I hear you, and you are right." At first, the story sounds comical and nonsensical. When you look deeper, what the Rabbi was trying to say is we all have a point, and there are no absolutes. When we can be thankful for this and allow it, we get to connect in the sheer joy of being. We are all here, being. With points of views, beliefs, losses, great happiness, gifts and with trauma. We are all here, being, and it alone connects us with no one having to be wrong.

There is no set rule–book, and there is often no guaranteed logic surrounding how events will play out. No matter what, we get to choose gratitude for the things we can control and for the things we can't, for the specific attention each person in our life desires, and for the ways that attention lets connection bloom. Feeling heard and seen and coming from a place of love will never lead us astray. Isn't that what gratitude is? Hearing and seeing what is good now and loving it?

Dwelling on or ruminating about what doesn't work out, what we didn't get, what isn't happening the way we want when we want it, and what isn't ours in this lifetime will never bring us contentment, and it will also never bring us real connection. Finding a way to stay grateful – whether through a gratitude list or prayer, mindfulness or the people whom you choose to spend time with, it will open you up to others, and then you will never be alone. You will never be a failure or unlucky, for you will be too busy counting your blessings and soaring high because of it. Birds like that usually naturally find a whole flock to fly with.

Unconditional love is unconditional gratitude. Having that skill, where you can find the silver lining in anything, is one of the most charismatic ways of walking through this world. Reflecting on the good you already have going on in your life will bring you more people to reflect with and more joy when reflecting. Sure, it entails a knack for turning tragedy and suffering into an opportunity. Sure, it entails a finesse in positive thinking in negative circumstances or experiences. This ability will bring forward the people you can be honest with, share the good, bad, and ugly, and get back non–judgmental, loving guidance in return. This is how you create an endless loop of things to be grateful for, a happy life, and a circle to share it with. As the great Rumi said, "being human is a guest house." Every experience and emotion come with lessons and guides. We must invite everybody in.

Question for You

How grateful can we be to be part of something? How grateful can we be to be one of many? How grateful can we be a point of connection in this world, like a giant game of telephone where there is someone on either side of me and you, and the chain keeps going?

Being thankful is the most magnetic, fastening bind between people. Once we see through a grateful lens for ourselves, we can use that same lens for others, and then they can use it for us. Then, we all want each other to succeed, to celebrate, to win, to give thanks for what we have. And we want to do it together. Appreciating your life – from the small things to the big things – will not only bring you joy, it will also connect you to everyone in your life because they will be beings you are thankful for. And we feel that, don't we? When someone looks at us, treats us, and counts us as a blessing. I encourage you to keep a gratitude journal, or to jot things you're thankful for down on the back of a crumpled receipt if you must. That will be enough. Just start to notice what you appreciate, and watch as more things to appreciate come flooding into view and into your life.

PART TWO

WHAT YOU DO

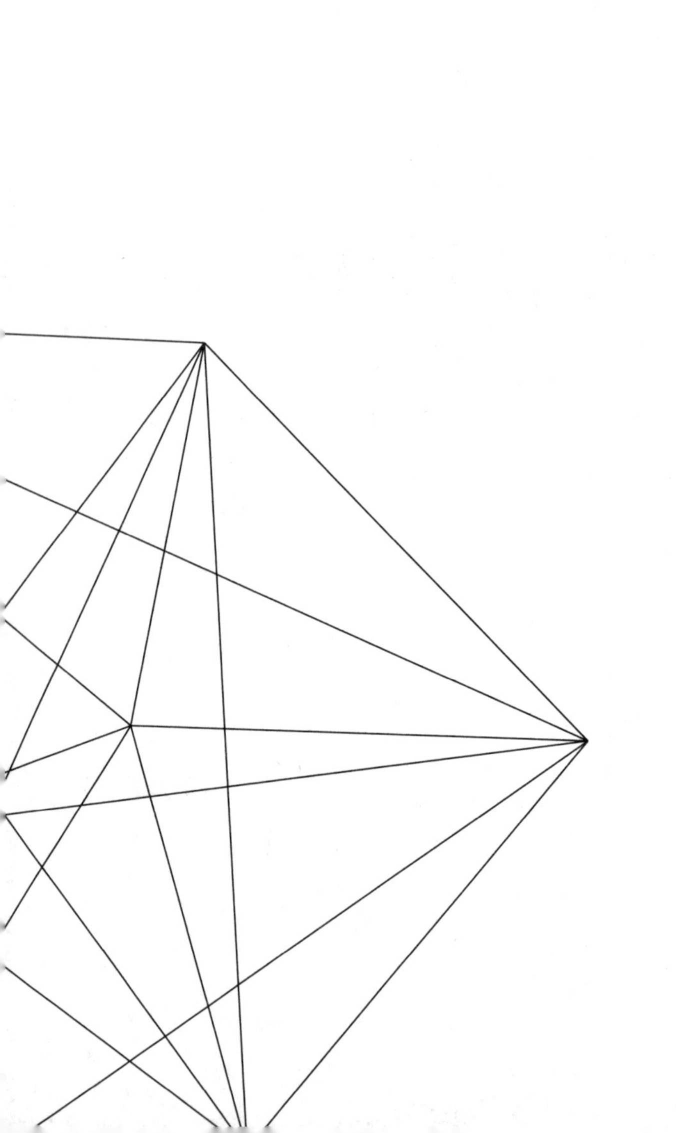

We have talked about our beliefs, what is between our ears and the basis of our lives. Beliefs are thoughts we tell ourselves repeatedly, and so addressing them first is key for rewiring ourselves back towards connection. From that place, from that more open, willing place where we can see a mountain we've been looking at from a window as different because we stood up, went outside, and no longer stared from the same window and same seat but walked around it, dared to expand our perspectives and our beliefs – from here we can begin to DO. What do you want to do? What doing will bring you more connection? As they say in the 12 Step rooms: "Faith without works is dead." So you gotta get up and go do something.

What we do not only entails being of service, which I referenced in the previous pages as something to believe in, but also what we do assembles ourselves as conduits of connection, even as hosts for connection. Hosts who invite connection in for an indefinite stay. We do this through what we give by, how we act and what we put out there. We do this by what we give to ourselves and how we act and what we take in. How we treat ourselves. Our actions must be reframed and it must start with the intention to connect, inside and out, so that connection is wholeness in the world.

You may have noticed that I call the sections of this book "conversations," and as we move now from what we believe to what we do, I'd like to unpack why. As an addict in recovery, like certain drugs or behaviors can be the gateway into an addiction, so can certain conversations be a gateway into connection. I wouldn't dream of editing the already wonderful structure that is the 12–Step program so there is no need for more steps or alternative steps beyond the twelve, as far as I am concerned. I am concerned with identifying individual portals, entry ways, points of access so you, me, all of us can find and enter a more connected, cohesive life. I have found that beliefs alone, my thoughts and internal life, though essential to address and to elevate, though essential for the health of my mind, heart and spirit, aren't the whole kit and kaboodle when changing. I have also found that it is who I am regarding the actions I take, the way I move in the world and interact with others in the world, this begins to bring me closer to the doorways I am seeking and to pure connection itself. What I do takes me beyond what I am living into something more satisfying that exists within the dynamics of implementation, application, and conversation.

We can always grow in our connections and become more connected. This work never ends, and that may be the greatest fact of the human condition, for once we have "arrived" or know it all or are done and all the boxes are checked, then we might no longer need God, one another, or to be alive. Being alive is an act of continuously, consistently pursuing connection.

In this conversation of the book, let's focus on how we perform, execute, show up, and move energy through life to achieve connection. The reality of doing good brings about more feeling good in a full–bodied, three–hundred–sixty–degree way. So, as we do what we do, the hope is that our gateways become clearer, more visible, and more accessible to walk right through and into the rest of our bursting, beautiful, webbed–together lives.

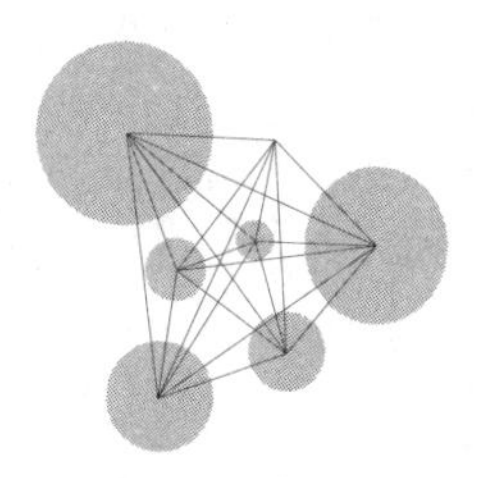

Conversation Ten: From Complicated to Simple

We are born into enoughness. Somewhere along the way we are taught, shown, and told that the mundane is not beautiful, that the ordinary must become extraordinary, and we atrophy the practice of enjoying the simple in life. The joy of making food, gardening, cleaning, tending to your space, conversing in the present with nobody anywhere else able to send you a message that pops up on a screen. A simple life is all we need; it's all we've ever needed. It's how we were designed. Then technology and commerce and trade grew like giants.

If you want more and then still more, go for it. But if you're reading this book because you are lacking connection, I'd like you to entertain the notion that all the stuff and accolades and fancy upgrades around you will not be what fills up or fastens you to others in the name of constructing more love. Often, when we turn to the avenues of illusion and surface, we get further pulled away to what matters and what has meaning, which can be found most efficiently and potently within the freedom of a simple life of doing. Your hands in the dirt.

What does that mean – simple? It has this bad connotation, doesn't it. Why? Simple means humble. Simple means natural. Simple might be more of a feeling than a definition, like you're lying in a hammock or rocking on a boat that cannot get lost. It means unassuming, not pretentious, back to the basics. It means less noise and clutter, consumption, and production so we will hear and see, taste and feel the essence of what lights us up and what is with us right here, right now. It's hard enough to ever seem like anything other than minimal when we overcomplicate our lives with the insatiable, complex, knotty misbeliefs that more outside of us will save the rotting tangle inside of us.

I had a fascinating conversation with my 11–year–old daughter the other day. She told me that her classmates and teacher were discussing their relationship with God and his commandments. Her friends said that they must observe the commandments, otherwise, God would be angry with them, and so they feared God. My daughter told them: "God doesn't want you to be scared of him, rather he wants you to know that he loves you and is guiding you with his commandments. If you are only following a commandment because you are afraid of God, I don't think God wants you to perform the commandment at all." My first thought was, "WOW! My daughter has a brilliant mind!"

Then it hit me that as I grew up—and even still today—I began to form a more complicated relationship with God. It didn't start that way for me as a child, just as it didn't for my children. And I don't want to be a force that tarnishes that for them, that convinces them of the byzantine requirements of a less simple life, where even spirituality is burdened by complexity and hoop–jumping. I want my kids to understand God as a Father in heaven who loves them more than any being can ever love anyone, who wants us to live our best life, whose love is as organic and easy as breathing. If they accept that as an alignment—if I don't show them through my spiritual malady otherwise and whack them out of alignment—then simplicity is all they need for they already have everything they need inside of them.

God is connection. Connection is God.

God is in us. God is every one of us.

Whether or not fearing God is healthy for you, I'll leave it for you to decide. This power greater than you can be the most important relationship in your life so does fearing it help or hurt the relationship? Misconceptions of God can disconnect us and harm us more than anything else. God does not have to be demanded of you by others or demanding of you as a conditional ruler to fear, and if you were taught to believe that, I am so sorry. One of the most beautiful things about the 12–Step program is the encouragement to not only create your idea of a Higher Power, the kind you would want to give your life and will over to, but to build a life around that Higher Power and know they got your back. In that light, God and faith are beautiful, personal elements that make life rich and full no matter what you have. God as the simply good force you need to whom you can whisper, Be with me. It is intrinsic to who you are, I'd argue, the lowest hanging fruit, not sophisticated but clean and plain and unadorned, to participate in this act of personal imagination. For me, this served to anchor the idea that my needs being met, and my basic core values tended to was all I ever wanted, and anything that will pull me away from that or dazzle me into thinking otherwise was just too great of a risk to my connection with truth, with God as I understand God.

Rabbi Jonathan Sacks said: "Love is the highest of emotions." For me, forgoing my terror of God and the worry that the divine will take what I had away from me if I did not do exactly what God wanted and instead landing on a vision of an unconditionally loving God I had to do nothing to please, proved to be the basis for my life. Everything stems from there. What if God already approves of me and of you? What if God's love is not a business deal, not restricted or qualified, not complicated, but rather inherently reciprocal and free–flowing? What if the simplest actions you take in your life are the touchstones to feeling this most? That is how I love other people and myself. That is what makes connection possible.

Love does not have to be fraught with danger, fickleness, performing for favor, disdain or withholding because another didn't do what I wanted them to do. God doesn't have to love me like that, either. I don't have to distract myself with more things, either. True love does not separate us at all but holds us constantly. Love is simple. Are there areas where you can surrender the hobby of chasing more for the grand embrace of the simplest things? What if the minute we need to prove our lack and justify buying more, we begin to deteriorate and not connect but compete and turn away from God? It is the basis of all crime, I believe—the division of us, the inhumanity and dehumanizing beliefs that are born out of the lie that a web of stuff can replace the simplicity of a Higher Power.

I was asked once to help a man whose grandfather targeted and committed crimes against Jewish people. Before agreeing to, I wondered about how to find sameness between people who have been blinded by separation before. I wondered how to find a middle ground with someone you disagree with on the big issues. I ultimately said yes to the arrangement because I realized how simple morality and virtue are, and so the question I went into these conversations asking myself was: Does love have to be so complicated? Is love complex by its very nature? And if so, then how do we get through it? How do we show up for it? Shall we even show up for it?

Helping this man brought me the knowledge that there can exist distinctions between our political, economic, and religious beliefs, but that we can still adhere to humanity despite those differences and despite them. Humanity is the simple core we all need to adhere to, and we are meant to stay with it. Humanity is achieved through doing. Humanity is connection, in action. We are all seeking safety and connection. Unfortunately, we usually go about it in ways that end up killing us. We can live for it instead of die for it.

Your thoughts and beliefs can be what they are, but your behavior has the power to connect you regardless, maybe even to bump up against, challenge, and dismantle the thoughts or beliefs that venomously divide you from somebody else or worse yet, justify in your mind why you should hurt them. Despite the family and social circumstances we are born into, we all share the same basic needs and the same pool of consequences. When those needs are not met, our hurt and pain will manifest in similar veins. Yes, we are all that simple. That brought me back to what was straightforward and essential as it pertained to the man whose family contributed to the suffering of my people and community. I want God to love me always and forever, and He does. And so I reminded myself that I can love this person too, always and forever. It was a blessing to love him. A privilege and a pleasure. It was one of the simplest things I've ever one—not easy, but simple because it reminded me who I was born to be. And it remains one of the most powerful acts of connection I have ever been part of. We can build a network that actively operates on simple principles. We can let that be enough.

The difficulty I endured engaging with a man who disagreed with me so vehemently was complicated, but the compassion and common ground we discovered during our discussions was simple. It became a space we shared that held room for both of us. This is how we get closer to safety and connection for all, to the world we all dream of. And I know that the way I restructured my formerly complicated relationship with God had everything to do with how I showed up for this man. I became the extension of the God I believe in, the unconditionally loving and forgiving one, the kind one, the one who listens. It brought me closer to Him.

Question for You

I'd like to invite you to take a sheet of paper and fold it in half. On one side, consider your faith and belief system around a power greater than you, and write down what comes out when you reflect on that power. Then, on the other side, take a moment to jot down everything you already have. Do you feel that your life is simple or complicated? Do you constantly crave more or feel burdened by having too much? Now, unfold the page and look at the two sides. Is there a correlation there? Are there connections to be made about the terrain of connection within you?

Be curious, remain nonjudgmental, for this is not a gotcha exercise designed to shame you. This is about listening to your responses and learning from the child still inside of you—the one who grew up to be the person reading this book. The one who knew what enough felt like in terms of a lifestyle and how adjusting those knobs can take us away from the feeling of union we actually crave most. Consider what you might need out of a Higher Power and how natural it might be to decide that God exists in your life, in the simple day–to–day activities.

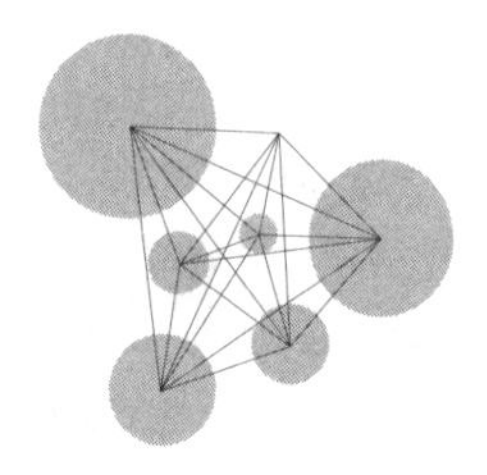

Conversation Eleven: From Scarcity to Generosity

The Bible tells us a wild story about ten men, all of status, humility, and integrity. These men are respected by all as devout and faithful to God and were chosen to check out the promised land of Israel and report on their findings. Instead of returning and reporting positively or accurately, they reported with negativity—slanderous and exaggerated negativity of the land. This forced Moses to never enter the land of his heart, and resulted in the people of the Bible being stalled in the desert for a considerably longer amount of time. What happened?!

Rabbi Sacks talks about the great Sage, The Chabad Rebbe, and explains that the ten men, the Spies as they were called, were not afraid of failure, which is commonly thought; rather, they feared success. They weren't afraid that they might fail in a land they couldn't live and thrive in, they were afraid that spiritually, they would be better off in the desert where all was provided for them. They were afraid that the distractions of success would prevent them from being the best they could be. But God doesn't desire for us to stay in a desert or in a forest to isolate ourselves. We do not need to have less to serve God more. God wants us to sanctify, to make our houses peaceful so the spirit is comfortable resting there. God also wants us to treat others with love as beacons of happiness and hope, to share and grow together. It is through creating communities of generosity that participate as well as give to one another, it is by building collective circles, that scarcity becomes an impossiblity.

Don't mistake isolation, self–punishment, or restriction as a form of spirituality. Do not confuse having more with anything less than being able to give more with greater generosity. Don't act modestly to stop from creating jealousy amongst your fellows. Be happy with what you have! Be charitable and bighearted with what you have! Be proud to enjoy the plentiful, and celebrate what is rich in your life because spirituality is abundant! It is joy if it is shared with others. Spirituality depends on me, yet it manifests when I give to you.

A sneaky trend encourages us to feel shameful about what we have and to hide giving too much when nothing can be further from the point. How can we share something we feel bad about? How can we even achieve more of something we think is inherently evil or wrong? Why would we? A scarcity mindset does not make you a better person.

Limiting yourself is a fake shield, and it will not curb envy or jealousy from others for what you have or don't have. Austerity will not necessarily help you connect. It may not be God's plan for you to renounce your wealth in whatever form it comes. God is unlimited and provides for all of us and can give every single person abundance without taking from anyone else. God wants each of us to be dancing graciously over our bounty so we can share it with others. Once we accept this, connection is so much easier, and so is receiving what is meant for us.

Now, showing off is a desire to make yourself feel better than others, and that is a surefire way to prevent connection and create bitterness. Welcoming others to participate in the goodness you offer, though, that is not bragging, that is inviting; bragging has an intention of cutting us off from one another, but sharing comes from knowing the wonders of a gift and wanting to distribute it so more people can enjoy it, trusting you will only enjoy it when they do too. In the Jewish tradition, we are instructed to repeat the story of the exodus from Egypt every year and remember it daily. God delivered the Israelites from slavery, provided the Law, and gave instructions on how His people can be made holy.

On the annual commemoration of Passover, we are instructed to tell our children the story and its significance. We know that we are instructed to share these stories—but why? Because children are the future and educating them is the key to making sure the future is fruitful for all because wisdom is abundance, too. To be more specific, teaching children where they come from, and their shared stories gives them a greater sense of identity and the confidence to reach their potential because they have within them the generous cushion of history. It is free. It is copious in its lessons. It is to be communicated, revealed, savored, and passed along. This is the power that makes even our struggles an act of generosity that connects us, links us in learning and acknowledges scarcity as a traffic sign towards progress, towards potential.

Because life entails some suffering, it is true. I have had my share of personal struggles. Our struggles need to be shared because this is how we realize that we don't walk alone in our suffering. By sharing our stories, we let others tap into the belief that they may overcome whatever challenges they may be going through, and vice versa. Generosity is an outlook that fastens us to one another, not only in terms of the good stuff we have but also including the negative and the difficult. Sharing stories generously lets others have an internal library of what to do shall the time come. It allows others to strategize and apply information, and it connects them to us, and us to them. Being generous about all of our life experiences and about all of who we are is the most spiritually rewarding thing we can do. I ask you now: Is there something you can share today? A story of recovery, a meal at your table, extra clothes, the gratitude you feel—these are just some examples. Where can you give more? Where is abundance raining down on you, that may be the area somebody else needs watering?

I promise you if you go out with the motivation to reveal and bond, to be known and to know others, your life will transform into a hub of connections inside of you and outside of you. You cannot feel lonely if you live this way. What I have to come to understand is that within this internal awareness, I can appreciate everything as a gift I have been given and then share all the gifts with those around me. Generosity is not only an action of connection, it is also an inspiration to behave as if your burdens and your festivities, the spilling forth of your cupboard of library or laughs or loss, all of you is for everybody to partake in. This erases the mythology of our separateness. From there, we realize that connection is the method which we actively distribute and redistribute to return home.

Giving to charity is a regular part of spiritual life. I'd argue that it is part of most religions and most people because we are wired to donate what we can—and no amount is too small—to those less fortunate than we are. Though I can only speak confidently about this regarding biblical law, I hope it will shed some light on its value. The scripture commands that we give ten percent of our income but not greater than twenty percent in some charitable way. I believe deep in my soul that if everybody gave ten percent of their income to the needy and to the infirm, we wouldn't have the needy and infirm anymore. And so it's not God that must come to our rescue, it's us who must come to our rescue by being generous with our riches, whatever level those riches may be.

I had the honor of officiating at the funeral of a gentleman who lived for 94 years and enjoyed a full life. He was a veteran of the Navy and a professional boxer. He'd adopted and raised 3 children as his own, so much so that I didn't know they were adopted until the day of his funeral. And above all else, this man was charitable. What is remarkable about this gentleman is that I remember that when I was around seven years old, he had a Lamborghini. He'd offer all the kids in the neighborhood rides, and we'd laugh, windows down, screaming in delight at being in a Lamborghini! He uplifted the material by recognizing that he was merely a custodian of it, that his job was to share it joyfully instead of having it for its own sake. He made even a fancy car soul-centric due to his perspective and intention, keeping a level head, which I believe must be practiced through our efforts. Above all, he was generous about his luxury car. All the hard work that had paid off as nice things didn't matter as much to him as the resilience and guts and discipline he learned by working hard to make a good living. The car was just something to let kids into so they can feel the wind in their hair and smile beside him.

The people at Lamborghini-man's funeral never mentioned how much money he had. He took none of his "stuff" with him when he died. But his memory—what he left behind—was so full of wild giving that it had me contemplating as one often does after a funeral. I pondered the importance of living a generous life and reflected on what will be my legacy. I kept thinking about what one of my teachers, Ted, said about a tree. He explained that for many years, we focus on the trunk, which is our ego: who and what we are in this world, where we belong, how much we have, how important we are, and so forth. At some point, that stops working, and we focus upwards on the branches, which are various forms of spirituality, meditation, prayer, and the activities of the day that can elevate our lives. Ultimately, when that isn't enough by itself, that's when we focus on the roots, which is our soul. When I go inwards to my soul, I know that if I lived in accordance with my soul, money would not count for much, and status wouldn't either, but my impact would. When I reach for my soul, I feel the eternal life that will stay after I pass, which is embodying peace, which I will share liberally with the world to feel.

Question for You

We must be God–like in our living so that God is already here. God has set up solutions through tithing to nudge us forward and all we have to do is merely strive to fulfill our part of the bargain.

Ask to where or to whom to be generous to? Answer this question deep in the limits of your spirit. Ask yourself what your priorities are and give to champion that cause. Coupled with the many ways to vet organizations, all giving is good giving, as it is possible to make sure most of the funds you give go to people and programs, not overhead.

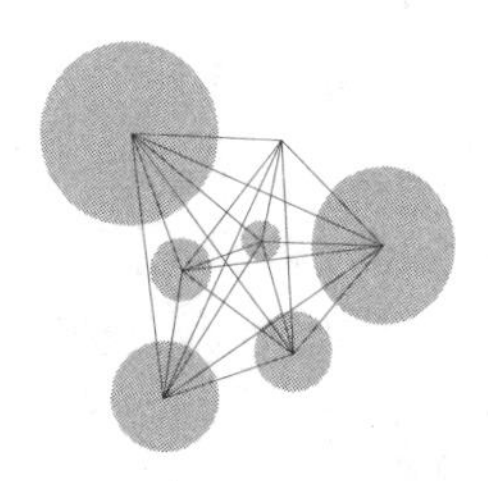

Conversation Twelve: From Demanding to Receiving

We live in a world that tells us to hold on to what we have. To hold on tight and still tighter. This line of thinking makes us believe what we have not only can, but definitely will, get stolen by others, by the government, by God, or that you can make a dumb move and lose it all, that you have to be ten steps ahead and outsmart what is coming after you. This line of thinking makes you think you don't have enough, there is never enough, and you're not there yet. This mentality was designed on purpose to keep us spending money and collecting things while assessing what we have, what we don't, and comparing ourselves in the never–ending question of why others might have more, which makes us demand more. Someone else will always have more. And someone else will always have less. It is impossible to be in connection with a Higher Power and your Higher Self or with others, if you are consistently feeling short–changed and insistent.

The things you want—the things you are commanding to be yours – are already present, you merely have to line up your vision of what is to receive them. This is the basis of every 12 Step program that we open our palms and let it come in instead of living a life of grabbing desires. What you demand has a *feeling* attached to it, an energy—whether or not you get "the thing," that feeling and energy is already here! You can let yourself receive it now! This at the source of connection in general.

I am not insinuating or suggesting you become a martyr or a doormat or a slacker, giving up all wishes until you basically cease to exist because you sit and wait for some magical force to pump up your balloon to its fullest while you go on and deflate. I am insinuating and suggesting that you adopt a foundational concept and attitude that has saved my life and the lives of millions of other people, which is that we actually only get what we want by surrendering our demands so we can receive the goodness already in existence. This is how healing and recovery work. You don't have to "do" anything anymore. Nothing out there will fill us. We do less, let it come, and trust that our beings are pulled up into connection. The only reason for material goods is for the feeling and energy they provide. The goods themselves are rarely as valuable as the feelings they induce. Thinking the stuff will give you the feeling means you've bought into the lie; it's the other way around. The feeling is everything, and the material is a bonus.

Once we open our hands and stop requesting and stipulating with no strings attached, it means we now have open hands to get what is gracious, to attract what is meant to be ours. There is room now, we have made the space for the Universe to give to us again, which is not a miracle we can plan, predict, give a deadline for, or control. The act of receiving is an act of faith and grace, and it calls on us to always be looking–as if we typed it in a Google search bar–for what wonderful thing Source has given to us. Receiving where we were once pleading brings about a sense of connection because from this place everything feels like a gift already, and we are a magnet for more to be drawn to us as we become experts in receiving.

The space made by giving up our requirements shows everything that is already ours. The Universe can then feel our gratitude, see how we're noticing, and bless us again, for we receive so easily and enjoy so well! This is how we live a life not all about us or for us but steeped in the hopeful fact that every tree gets enough rain somehow, every flower, every shrub and so we do too. From this mindset, we care enough to embrace the easy flow of in and out and receive what is already here for us, which is connection. From here, we don't focus on what we are tantruming for more of, for we are too busy receiving the treasure of what already is.

We need not demand a thing when we live this way. We become vessels of appreciation, welcoming in a steady pattern of rain for our blossoming. Because the Universe is always giving to us, and our spirit are made to be wide open to receive those gifts graciously. And it makes us so gleeful! This is how connection multiplies and takes over our lives with a sense of more–than–enoughness that can only manifest when we believe in it and act according to it. When the hands are open, not hoarding or clutching, but allowing for more to come in, how natural life is to celebrate. It is joy we have to strive to most allow ourselves to feel, which only comes when we constantly forgo petitioning and instead get on with receiving.

I amassed so many things in my adult life—money, relationships, material items—and they left me broken into a billion pieces. I demanded more relentlessly, and I was never satisfied. It was a tall order, even unfathomable and worse, terrifying, to shift myself in away from demanding. Every part of my life is now built on the cornerstone of connecting to what is already here and it makes me realize that I do not need to want. I did this through the literal and metaphorical act of opening my fists again and again to less banging, and more openness.

Ironically, this new way of being in the world and with myself in the world wasn't something I had to work hard to accept. It happened as I became willing. I leapt. I jumped into it because I had nothing left to lose. I flung open my heart and disrupted the emptiness of persistent discontent. And I looked for the rewards life was showering upon me, and I expanded myself consciously to receiving them and being thankful for them. And because this perspective alone lifted my life so much, connected me to nature and God, myself and others, especially in such stark contrast to how I'd been living prior, I taught myself to believe that everything meant to be with me was coming because it wouldn't be able to miss me. I found the evidence every single time of how it comes and how it's already here. I focused on the fruits of glory now. It sounds like I thought it all into changing, but

I didn't. It was in the doing: I said goodbye to consistently needing and calling for more to be okay. It is a ritual for me still to say goodbye again every morning to remind myself – sometimes in prayer, sometimes I write it down, sometimes I bury something in my backyard. Do it however you want to do it. The point is we don't have to demand anything from the Universe when we are a conduit for everything in the Universe. When we know how to tap into the feelings and energy around us now.

I'd like to acknowledge that this shift may be harder for some, and if so for you, please know that it's in the practice of this outlook repeatedly that it becomes integrated and part of your psyche. If that discipline, the participation in a spiritual boot camp, is the path you need, I guarantee it will be more than worth it because you can be a channel for in-flow and outflow. One helps with the other. No stockpiling, no watchfulness, not taking, not feeling entitled to more as if the more you get then, THEN, you will feel the way you want. You feel the way you want first, and then you receive it in form the way Universe wishes to send it to you! It is an in–and–out reality. We create the feelings we want through co–creation because we can only create by being connected, by being a facilitator of moving energy. You will become spiritually stronger, and this will give you the biggest gift, which is that others can lean on you to build their soul–receptive muscles. Others will connect to you with ease. You will receive it. They will practice receiving with you.

Remember that the Ten Commandments were given and received, not chased down and not demanded. To receive is to soften and allow what comes when it comes. To take in. To let out desire. In and out, on and on, rinse and repeat, what a lovely cycle life can be as we change our mood and our lives by highlighting as if with a yellow marker every single moment we receive all the glory that is here for us, not taking any of it for granted, not asking for more, but experiencing the fullness, and then standing in that for others to. This richness can never be taken from us, and it enrichens our existence because we no longer need anything else. It is an act of self–love to live so connected and to receive because it feels good to receive. Receiving is the opposite side of the coin to giving. One makes the other possible, and they cannot subsist apart. To claim *I deserve to feel good* and then take the actions that allow in the good recognizes that we are here to live, love, and love living. We are not here to ask for more, expect it, and then keep asking.

Experience the shattering breakthrough of hearing a proclamation inside you that knows you have enough, knows you are enough, knows more is coming and knows you can receive it with such ease you don't have to worry, you don't even have to ask. This is how we take our life back. This is radical, rebellious, and revolutionary because it is the opposite of the system that's been designed to ensnare us, not because "they" are so terrible, but because we have diluted spirituality and chosen to focus on making money. Money and stuff will never, can never, satiate or even satisfy what you want, which can only come from spirituality, which demands nothing, which is the space inside you where you, funny enough, feel like you need nothing at all and are open to welcoming whatever comes.

We are made in God's likeness, so there is nothing to demand because we are not missing a thing. We deserve for life to feel like the leaning–back comfort of receiving instead of the hunching over the insistence of what we don't believe is coming, so we shout about it and chase it. No more. We open our eyes. We open our hands. We open our hearts. We are full.

Question for You

Receiving is an action, and it cancels out demanding. God wants to give us more so we can receive more and give more, and how generous God is.

Let's think about it now. Let's take a moment to journal. What are you insisting on in your life? What would you feel if you received the goodness of all the gifts you already have, in all their fullness? Is there a way you can let go of the demands you think will make you feel good even one percent more so you can feel good now and receive more because you already do? Nothing else should hinder needing to, running to, soak in the blessings that surround you. This is how we begin to nourish connection not only with Source and within ourselves but with others too, for we will embody the receiving mode. It is only a punishment to the one feeling that not yet are things right enough to stop needing more, not right enough to be happy. We get to feel good. We get to behave in ways that make us feel good.

Then, it may seem silly and irreverent but it's the quickest, easiest touchstone for receiving: Go for a drive with your kids, or your nieces and nephews, or your friends and their kids. Tell them to direct you. Tell them to get you lost. Watch their wonder and their excitement, their sense of adventure and spirit as they shout "Go left! Now right!" Receive the gift of joy, the suspension of belief you might find your way back by staying straight, and go with it. Let the playfulness wash over you. Maybe you will even roll down your windows. How good it feels when the cool air rushes towards you, to meet you. Let it in, let it in, let it in.

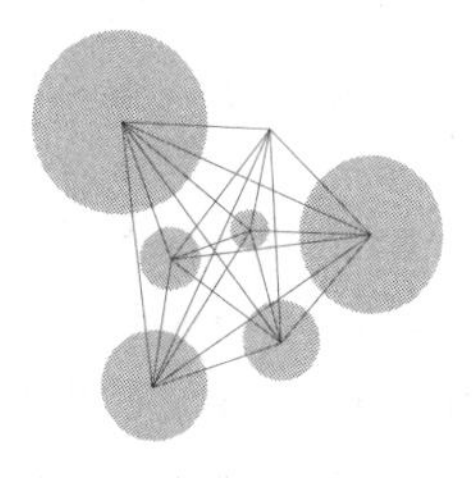

Conversation Thirteen: From Illusion to Invisible

I had a person say recently, "If God is omnipotent, then how is it that so many are struggling? Can't God come to our rescue just a bit?" Even in the observance of God—or shall I say, sometimes, especially in the observance of our religion—we can be naive and misguided. We want to not suffer. We want only good things to come from the choices we've made, but decisions have consequences, many of which we were aware of when we made them. As I like to say: We can't blow all our money at the casino and ask where God was. We shouldn't be playing our life savings at the casino. We cannot act irresponsibly and expect to be bailed out.

We can instead save our money. We can instead stay away from the gambling table. And if we can't, we can ask God to help us do so.

But not everything makes sense or has obvious repercussions to it. We cannot expect our human minds to understand the entirety of the Divine. We can only act responsibly and then remember that it's in God's hands, that God can always help us and is with us through whatever we face. Hope is not something we ever have to give up on. The key to life is that hope, living in connection to others, ourselves, and The One Creator. Hope is invisible and yet it is the realest sensation in the world. A tenet to living connectedly is this, moving from the illusion to the invisible. Illusion is everything we humans fall for. It's everything made of matter that's supposed to afford us a happily ever after. It's the deception of reality we defend and destruct. In the invisible, we must recognize that the world doesn't always make sense. The invisible is unseen but real, the realest thing in the world. We understand that we don't always understand. We make peace with the mysteries that will remain mysterious to us. We see that the world is more than what our eyes show – it is gracefully vast and unending.

I'd argue this is a doing and not a way of thinking because we have to strive to actively believe and hope, and we do that by betting on what we don't see, even when we don't always know why or how we'll do it. It is not our job to uncover and conquer every single corner of reality. It is our job to breathe into the bigger picture of what we don't know and let it all exist. It's not our job to hang onto the three-dimensional reality we can touch when the things that matter most are often invisible, like gravity and energy and love and connection. The illusion says it always adds up. The invisible is beyond sensible. It is sensed; it is trusted. This is how we expand our connection capacity because this permits us to show up for others in a deeper way. It lets us hold collective reverie for our smallness amidst a galaxy of vibrant frequencies. And it produces a type of connection that is both big and small, wise and unknowing, human and Divine. It lets us off our hook when we accept there is so much we will never comprehend, yet that is not a reason to disconnect.

There is a 14th–century author named Rabbi Moshe Luzato who wrote a book called *Pathway to the Just*. Love for the invisible is found in his profound words.

The Rabbi states that his book has nothing new. It is all concepts we already know and appreciate as beneficial to our lives, yet we don't practice them. He claims this is largely out of a lack of awareness, not because we don't believe in these ideals, but because we don't practice them. We don't hope for them through practicing them repeatedly, which is required to see beyond the horizon. The author continues to say that if you plan on reading his book once, then you might as well not start, as it won't penetrate and will make no difference in your life. By spending time with the book beyond first reading, beyond words so those words may spread, you're your bones, your blood, your actions, then and only then will souls remember that we comprise the same stuff that the universe comprises. From here, we can drop into a connection that is borderless and boundless, that is the whole wide cosmos.

I know this idea is obscure. I can own that! Still, please consider ushering in the ambiguities that are part of being alive, to go from buying into the illusion of what is made of matter and to connecting more with what is imperceptibly holding the world together. What we see is so seductive because it provides the illusion that nothing else exists. It blocks us from connecting, and it limits us.

I am reminded of a story of two brothers who survived the Holocaust: One of the brothers became an atheist, while the other remained a believer. These two brothers had not seen each other in many years and drifted apart, yet coincidentally ran into each other one day. The non–believer turned to his brother and stated, "After all of the horrible things we have seen and been through in this world, how can you still believe in God?!" To this, the faithful brother responded, "Okay, I must explain evil, which I cannot. You must explain everything else—the beauty in nature, the birth of a child, the workings of a human being, and you cannot. So how can you not believe in God?" The atheist brother was as stumped as the believer.

Illusion is a symptom of the ego and the limitations we've bought into. Connecting to the invisible is a symptom of understanding that even having faith in nothing, having faith that there cannot be a god, is faith... and so the brothers are more alike than not alike, both forced to reckon with the vagueness of what makes sense and the obscurities of being human. We connect with not having all the answers. We can choose to be connected to an atheist as a believer. We can be connected to the believers if we are atheists. The illusion tells us those two brothers are on opposite sides, that it's okay for them to feel superior towards each other because one of them is dumber than the other, but to both! Illusion is the root of disconnection.

Thoughts alone cannot widen our scope and cause us to act as parts of a whole. We must say yes to the invisible and actively collaborate with it, which requires us to listen to everything as equally true and untrue, not because we're looking for evidence or gotcha points, but because we're looking for connection spots. What an act of humble connection to hold an *I do not know.* To listen instead of dig in. To consider. To open to what we do not see. To say, "Huh, maybe." To let it serve us well. To let it serve us in connecting us in the unknown, together.

From here within, *I do not know* what is possible is infinite. From clinging to illusion, the offspring of materialism so easily wreaks havoc on our lives. There is nothing wrong with wealth, nice things, and enjoying life to the fullest, yet it can become a problem when it's the primary focus when we fail to recognize a reason for more within what we don't see. Money can become an obsession and cause us to forget how to be a good parent, a good friend, a good partner. Materialism is a selfish pursuit that relies on obtaining what can be touched, but it is the biggest illusion ever as it promises to give you everything and fills nothing. Now, my goal isn't to be a monk and it isn't to give up all material delights. That's an amazing virtue, it's just not mine. I choose to assign even the material with connection by acknowledging that I am nothing more than a trustee of everything in my orbit. As for, who I am for real? I try my best daily to act like the Soul I am who moves up and forward by working towards God, searching for the invisible strings that keep me tethered to God.

The challenges I have faced can be viewed as opportunities to push me taller and wider. I am grateful I have not been fooled into the trap of only paying attention to that which I can cut with a knife. All of that is an illusion, and it would cheat me out of a connection with the Divine, as well as with the Divine in me, which yearns to connect with the Divine in you. Inside the vast invisible, there is less positive or negative, fewer moods or attributes. There just is. There is an expansive isness. And there, we are all connected. We are all family. Become part of the stream of the unseen. Let yourself drown in the unending connection that is everywhere, even if it is undetectable by every sense other than the feeling one. You can behave as if you clearly see that to become part of life's plan, we must have faith in what we cannot see. This magnified, multiplied way of walking in the world will make you so bright that you will warm others as they sit by the fire of who you are, basking in your glow, which is eternal, which never goes out, which is not visible but constantly felt as a connection point.

It is brave, isn't it, in that Indian Jones scene where he steps a foot at the edge of the cliff and voila! A bridge appears. That is an action of connection, not thinking good things to manifest. It is a step out, a step that echoes repeatedly out because energy is that far–reaching and so potent that it makes a bridge out of wood real. Jones is not seduced by illusions of death or even of treasures. He sees beyond. We are here to take one step at a time as an homage to the immeasurable power that comes from the certainty of all that is real and invisible.

Question for You

If we can't prove something, then why not choose the idea that makes us feel better and helps us connect further? If it can help everybody lucky enough to share this unanswerable riddle of a planet with us, then why the hell not?! Think about something you are unsure of, something that has as many questions to it as answers. Wherever there is mystery in your life, what will it look like not to rush an ending, not to finalize a conclusion, but to instead live inside the mystery itself?

What makes you feel better? You get to choose that – it's enough of a reason.

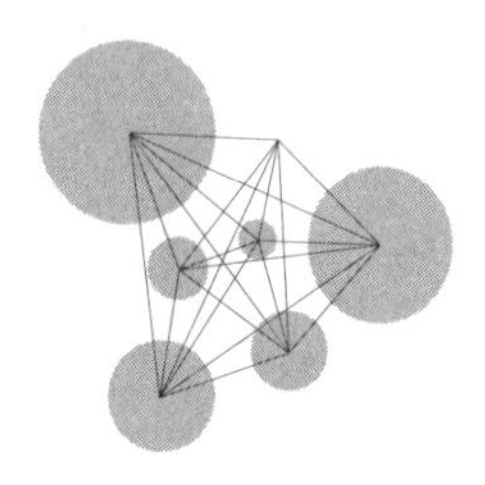

Conversation Fourteen: From Perfection to Growth

We must know and see others as they are, for who they are, and be aware of how our words and actions impact them. This is the most valuable benevolence we can ever model, and it is priceless. It is not, however, perfect. Because perfect does not let us know another or be known by them. Perfect is a separation, a façade, a cover and it prevents us from being close to one another. We always fail in the game of perfection.

During the Jewish holiday of Purim, which is similar to Halloween, we dress up in costumes and wear masks. These external masks represent the masks we wear daily as humans who choose to not reveal who we are. Masks we don for Purim remind us of the not tangible but just as real masks we have learned to use to present a perfect picture to the world that isn't in congruence with our soul–based values or our honest state of being, which is, in its essence, imperfect. My mask is commonly one of confidence, happiness, and making it seem as though I have it all together. But this mask hides my fear of asking for help along with my fear of needing anyone so deeply that they may hurt me if they rejected me. Throughout my darkest periods, I would never take off my mask and show myself to someone. I didn't do things to breed connection because I was too busy focusing on the protection of perfection. Protection and perfection are twins of discord. Just like drugs and alcohol are short–term solutions to long–term problems, as any immediate gratification is, perfection feels good to employ in the moment, but it robs us of connection.

There is no such thing as a shortcut without hard work attached. Overnight success takes about twenty years. The hard work that leads to success—and success is interchangeable with recovery—is imperfect, messy continuum of connecting again and again. The same is true for perfection in a way – the hard work that leads to the best version of ourselves is an imperfect, messy process of growing and growing again imperfectly.

I am not saying we should tell and show everything to everyone, but I am saying that every single person will have a journey of recovering from something precisely due to our imperfections and that this sweet spot is where we are the same. As a person in recovery, I have often struggled with transparency. The question is, what part of my story and my personal exploits do I share with the world, and with those closest like my children? And when do I share my story with them, when is the right time, and when is it inappropriate? I'd like to think those answers are found case by case, per individual, but I'd also like to think that those answers always include removing the masks we use. There is no protection when aiming for transparency – transparency allows for imperfection and blesses it as it vulnerably opens us up to connection.

This is what everybody wants: the intimacy and rawness of somebody who is see–through–real. So hiding your true self from others is counterintuitive, and it will only attract other hiders to you. An inflexibility to be known heralds a tendency to discount, and it reflects back more disconnection. The difference between a growth mindset and a fixed mindset can make or break how much you enjoy your life then and how close you feel to others. Because there is no need to be perfect when you're growing; when you're growing, you're making peace with the meaning of life, which happens not linearly, but in spirals, in little movements up and back that swirl endlessly around itself. That fluidity is the fuel of connection itself because there is so much grace in the organic expansion and contraction of progress. Subscribing to a rigid, right–or–wrong lifestyle that is perfect one way or another constricts our choices and keeps what we do within a tight box of narrow options. It's black or white. This counts, but this doesn't.

True growth arrives nowhere. That's why it is connecting. True growth accepts anyone, and it does not use anything as an excuse to disconnect. Through the lens of growth, everything that has ever happened is valuable. What has happened to you or not happened to you is grounds for getting to know somebody else. Most people do not change unless they are forced to. It need not be that way. We need not wait until our backs are against the wall and the wall is on fire. We don't have to suffer and be pushed into it. We don't have to struggle to connect. We can choose to change. We can notice and grow. We can let the cautionary tales of others' lives and our past serve as an impetus to connect now and let it be easy and fun and natural and messy.

People in recovery, whether that be from substances, trauma, or what have you, are interested in transparency because they often feel the need to release into the world their shame, their pain, and their inventory. A word here about what you reveal throughout your growing travels: it can be extraordinarily selfish and harmful as well as counter to the principles of connection to share for YOU instead of relating for THEM. That's the bottom line, to check in with your intention and consistently ask yourself: *Why am I telling this tale?* That question is essential to answer before speaking and let it guide you as humanly and honestly as you would divulge to your therapist, sponsor, rabbi, kids, or friends. Because our actions affect others, and sometimes even our secrets aren't our secrets to tell. Sometimes, our growing is about what we don't share, not to seem perfect, but because it is sacred, or necessary to protect *them*. Using our own stories as vehicles for connection and not for self–seeking motives is an area to pay special attention to because speaking our stories, especially as they pertain to what we have overcome, can give others the courage to heal their narratives. The act we use to connect can become a cause for disconnection when it is all about us, for us, and although beyond perfection, still not beneficial to those we share with.

Considering our own family and thinking through how divulging may affect them will let us be led by the vulnerability we wish to employ, but also by a thoughtfulness to the reality that our journey impacts other people too. Connection must be weighed between opening up and keeping quiet sometimes – when to speak and bridge gaps for others and when to stay silent out of respect for the connections we have at home. This is how we grow – not perfectly or cleanly, but truly. Transparency is a tool for connection, it is not a carte blanche rule of law.

It is so tempting to slip back into old behaviors—no matter how unhealthy or destructive they may have been. Connection is a matter of moment–to–moment choosing, which involves the impossibility of perfection because not every moment is the same or requires the same from you, and our wellness or recovery or success must never be taken for granted. Connection is a growing thing. It demands reconnection with self, with God, and with life to bloom. We will not even get connection down perfectly.

After a horrible event like 9/11, there was a surge in kindness we showed to one another in our country, which was so beautiful to experience. Then life quickly went back to what we call "normal," including disconnection and discontent. It didn't—and still doesn't—have to be the case. If we don't exercise the change muscle every single day, keep growing and allowing ourselves to be flawed, we fall straight back into old patterns of pre–recovery, which I often think of as signs of spiritual sickness. God, then connection, is about the reaching, about the striving, about being guided out of perfection thinking so we can sync up with others. All our fallible natures make us need one another, make us need collective strength to keep loving. God perhaps wants us growing – it is the basis of our spiritual well–being. Ask an addict in recovery. Recovering addicts know this better than anyone: how to keep going one day at a time, imperfect but evolving.

In my journey, I have experienced many mini–crises along the way. These crises were God's way of guiding me back toward the path that my soul needed to find recovery, which always led me back to connecting with other people. Anytime we call for the impeccable and let that swell of hardness rise like a tide that takes us under, we have moved back into ego and out of Spirit. We have disconnected. We are unreachable. And so each crisis can only end when we move out of ego and back into Spirit to connect again. Consistent actions based on the permission for imperfect progress proudly highlight the flaws that brought us to pick up this book. These are our most incredible parts, whether others know it or not. We know it. Knowing it and growing it is how we will save one another's lives. This is how we build connected relationships that become the basis for the rest of our imperfect time here.

Question for You

Ask yourself now: How can you make permanent elements in your life more malleable, more adaptable, more imperfect, more shareable when appropriate, and keep them growing? Where can you shift from exactness to progress? A better way to treat one another, yourself, nature, and the myriad of life experiences is within the yielding softness of releasing rigid limits that demand perfection like shackles. The pursuit is the goal. The pursuit is the connecting tissue. The pursuit is cyclical.

Write this down. Write down how to keep growing love for yourself despite your mistakes. Maybe that's through daily prayer. Maybe it arrives in you when you meditate and sit in silence. Maybe it blooms by doing good deeds or by forgiving everyone for their mistakes, too. Offering grace to build it in yourself.

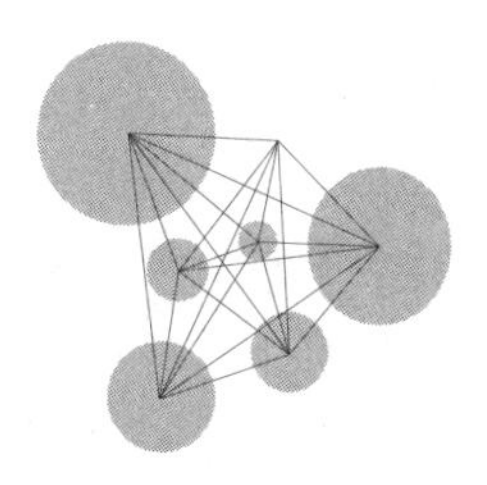

Conversation Fifteen: From Determined to Inspired

Competing drains us. Though determination is glorified in American culture, it has robbed us of what trumps it every time, which is inspiration. Inspiration can only come from connection. Determination comes from the lie that we can do it alone if only we focus and strive hard enough and figure it all out.

Do you remember the grave sin of the Golden Calf in the Old Testament? So the story goes of the Golden Calf (found in Exodus 32 in the Bible) that when Moses was away for too long, the Israelites asked Aaron to make them a new god. Aaron took their golden earrings and made a Golden Calf, which was an idol that the people worshiped instead of the Real God. Until they learned their lesson. The lesson is what makes it worthy of being in the Bible – it's a lesson so many humans still need to learn. What made Moses the greatest leader of his time and still to this day is that he led from humility and love, with proper boundaries, and with inspiration, not determination. According to the Bible, God told Moses he would destroy the people who built the Golden Calf, but Moses told God: "If so, erase me from your book, as I am nothing without my people." Moses didn't ask God to just save him or his family. Moses didn't sneak out alive while everybody else died. No, Moses asked God to save every member of his community because they were his family, too, and he was a vessel for them all, not just for himself.

Ambition can involve false worship. Dedication can be a Golden Calf. It tells us we don't need God, we don't need others when both a Higher Power and a people inspire us to do something that matters. They inspire us and are insured by us. Staying with these points of connection and both setting and reaching for our goals from there can never lead us astray, for it means the essence of the things we want are woven into those we do it for, and why we're here on Earth in the first place with the privilege to get to do it. We're not here to only rely on ourselves, nor are we here to only get ahead for ourselves. Leadership is the byproduct of inspiration precisely because it is all about how we can serve others, not about how they can serve us. Determination often becomes about being number one by whatever means necessary, no matter who is stepped on along the way.

As parents, we owe the ultimate example of leadership to our children. We can show our children who we wish them to be. Sit down with your kids and let them know their feelings and thoughts matter and will be considered. That they have value as a member of the board of directors of this family. Don't you want them to do that for others when they grow up? Through action, through remaining connected to them even when we mess up and even when they mess up, we will help them and ourselves metabolize the truth: that children must not love their parents no matter what. No, it is parents who must love their children no matter what. We will also be modeling for them. We will connect from our best selves to their best selves.

Parenting is not determination, not getting what we want, not being right, not being more important or wielding our in–charge power. It shall be an inspired role to be a parent, to lead by knowing you are for those children, and to love so there is always a path for them back to you. The days of being determined to make your kids who you want them to be are over. It only closes our door to them. Children are inspired sovereign beings, and the ways they challenge us are opportunities for more connection. This is what it feels like to live a life of jumping in the water to save our fellows, and especially our family, from drowning. We don't wait for them to flail or choke or sink, for we are so in sync that we are already there to offer our support. We pave the path back home to us and keep it lush and clear.

Gandhi famously said, "A small body of determined spirits fired by an unquenchable faith in their mission can alter the course of history."

Determination can be a helpful ingredient to a life filled with connection. It's just that the inspiration part, the faith part that is more powerful than our mere mortal brains and necessary to turn on determination as a force. Being driven from external factors and for external wins is a disconnected way of living. What makes a project or idea or career or relationship spiritual is the connection to its meaning, what it gives you and, more importantly, what you can give to it. It makes our art and endeavors spiritual in and of themselves. There is a quote that has had a huge impact on me: "Even if a knife is pointed at your neck, do not give up hope." I think that even people who have faced enormous suffering like severe sickness, imminent financial ruin, struggles with their children, and trauma, can be due to their undying faith combined with their determination to enjoy life overcome both their external and internal obstacles.

No matter how far the scale we go, we will always be better off maintaining an attitude of connection than those who give up hope, hide, or align with worry and fear. The power of positivity is remarkable, and what I'm concluding here is that perhaps it is made up of both determination and inspiration. Is there an area where you can use both? Is there a spot in your psyche that calls to lay down your sword, give up and retreat only to return with inspiration? I encourage you to mindfully build up your resilience and faith muscles when things are going well by breathing into the connective tissues in your life. With yourself, others, and your Source, be gentle and kind, be for the union and not just for the determined mindset of each for himself. Staying connected when things are good helps us feel connected so we can feel connected when things are <u>not</u> good.

Little things like looking people in the eye, listening and paying attention, sincerely asking how someone is and meaning it, smiling, these are always inspiring acts, and they're not so little. They let people know that we hear them.

This is what it means to be by another's side, to live a life where others are not alone, and you are not alone. Be determined to inspire. If you know someone who may need to hear it, let them know you are there with them. Your support could be enough to alter the course of their history.

Have you ever found that when someone is speaking to you—especially when their viewpoint differs from yours—while listening to them, you are crafting your response? Rather than listening to what the other person is saying and determining why they are saying it, we are often quick to go on the defensive or offensive, which prevents us from hearing the potentially valuable information being shared. The habit of not listening doesn't just happen when I'm around others – it's extra loud when I try to meditate or pray or hear God because I haven't practiced slowing down or staying hyper–present in the moment. The thoughts in our head can be enlightening and force us to learn how to listen – to ourselves, to God, to others. It's not that our thoughts are facts or even true. They lead to reflection and connection. Our inner voices need not cause us anxiety if we use the gift of listening. From here, as we learn to hear ourselves without judgment, we can do so beyond ourselves, like a ripple out. The skill is almost like interviewing feelings and thoughts and asking what they are trying to tell us and where they are guiding us to. Instead of being afraid and needing to either distract ourselves or respond right away, inserting that pause and allowing ourselves to gather information opens us up to true connection based on the simplest tool for it: listening.

Question for You

In conversation with others, is there a way to talk without the purpose of responding and instead actively strive to hear what the other person is actually saying? Not preparing, not determined to make your point, but instead sharing, collecting information, feeding the soul – yours and theirs? Not only will this be beneficial in your conversations and enhance their quality and quantity, it will also increase the level of connection you feel with others. Whether it's negative voices inside your head or others with opinions different from yours, whether the chatter is loud or soft, it is an act of inspiration from your Higher Self to hear it and engage without determination for your agenda or for the discussion to be anything other than what it is.

Self–determination—a right and privilege for all—is an inspired act. It is born out of listening and connecting. It keeps what can become a dogged, resolute matter stirred into an inspired reality. That is a connected action, which we must let God allow.

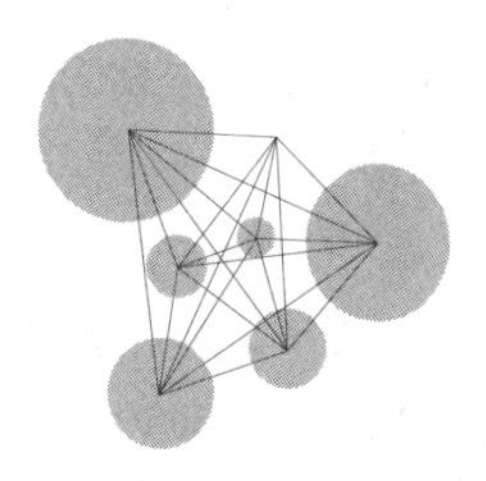

Conversation Sixteen: From Dependence to Autonomy

Victor Frankl said, "Everything can be taken from a man but one thing: the last of the human freedoms—to choose one's attitude in any given set of circumstances, to choose one's own way." Frankl emerged from one of the most tragic events of humankind – the Holocaust – with this philosophy. His lived tragedy inspired him to write "Man's Search of Meaning," one of the most powerful books ever written, and sprinkled throughout the pages are his lessons and enlightenments. This is the ultimate form of autonomy, he argues – your mind. You choose your psychology. Your way of looking at the world, the lens and filter you consciously or unconsciously pick up, to make sense of the world as a bounty of connection or as a place that's against you, it's your call.

When I reflect on the journeys from slavery to freedom, I question the constraints we continue to place on ourselves and others. Because how we treat ourselves is the baseline for how we treat the world. And the way we treat others only reflects how we treat ourselves inside, in that head as it lies on a pillow and talks in the dark to no one else. Negative thoughts dampen the spirit. Biases limit us. Steepening further into the role of victim continues to harm me because it either makes me feel resentful and helpless or moves me to oppress others to protect myself. That dichotomy will never die, that ying and yang.

Jews were enslaved in Egypt, while others all around the world lived freely. This happened with African Americans to an extent that is a shameful part of United States history and to various other groups. Since the dawn of time there has been the group being controlled, being made further dependent and held back and told what to do, while others dance to the tune of their freedom. And yet everybody has the opportunity to, in their minds, become liberated and to let that be the beginning of whatever that freedom can grow into. Mental freedom is more real than reality. It is connection.

I turn to the wisdom of Frankl again. We can easily slip into despair if we do not like our lives, or we can lean into a different emotion and take on a different perspective. Eventually, this too shall pass, they say, but disease and affliction can happen again. Possibly to one part of the world and not to another. Some will suffer while others are spared. This is life, and I don't know why, and I can't make sense of it. In either scenario, wherever you are on the wide range of experiences, you can choose to make sense of the world in whatever way you wish. This choosing is the ultimate liberty. Don't let anybody take it from you. The choosing is the connection. The choosing is an action, and it should involve your whole chest.

From that place, another's suffering is our own, as well another's joy. From there, we honor both and acknowledge our part as autonomous beings that are simultaneously independent from others and united as one. It's not about following through with the restrictions placed on us about who we should be, what we should believe and what camp we belong to. We guard the safety and well–being of others by guarding it in ourselves and vice versa, it is both externally and internally that autonomy leads us back together. It is about melting into the connected spot deep inside of us, in that bright overlap of mind, heart and spirit, where we are our own, only to discover we are inseparable. Unique. Connected.

This reminds me of birds and how they fly in flocks. They are individuals, yes, and yet they travel in groups. There's an obvious reason for this: more eyes and ears mean increased opportunities to find food and decreased chances of getting detected by a predator. Another reason is not that they have one group mind, because they actually do not; every individual bird is just that, an individual, and yet they respond to the movements of the other birds next to it. They impact one another because they are connected–not because of mob mentality–but because they influence one another as they work towards a common goal. Yet they are each their own and "choose" who they are. So it's not about being the same – for different birds even flock together! It is about being sovereign and working together. Being uniquely you're own bird, but working with other birds.

We, humans, have a common goal if we just let ourselves remember that: a safe and happy survival. We can continue to work together without becoming clones of one another, which squashes the beautiful authenticity inside each of us. That authenticity is what connects us – that we're each wholly and holy, unlike anybody else, when you combine all of our parts. We can coordinate efforts to make a great world for all and still be one of a kind.

Seeking connection is how we create safety, not by being replicas of each other. When we feel connected in healthy relationships and groups, we may change our minds, reach higher, think for ourselves, agree and disagree, but above all, honor the privilege to do so by letting others do so. Autonomy does not have to give way to fear. Homogeny is a product of fear. Insisting we all have to be the same, think the same, that is fear. That can only lead to dependence, not freedom. Autonomy is the most connective thread in the world because it combusts into a cocktail of respect and permission for individuality. Authenticity to have attachments, and not despite them, not attachments taken away because you want to be you, the singular you that shall be blessed in a group of singular others.

It is important to find this community—not needing to but welcoming the idea—because by the time that we *need* it, we usually feel alone, isolated in the head, and mired in more fear than we would like, having stayed in circles of dependence and homogeny by their nature disconnecting. It is ironic that the times we need people the most, we usually feel the most resistance to contact others. I'd argue that's because we've been used to forgoing our autonomy, which is the basis of all healthy relationships.

So yeah, if you lack community today, go take a workout class. That's my advice for a quick fix, not to become immersed in the group, for it's usually an hour–long class. But to begin to develop the identification of what it feels like to be YOU in a WE, so you'll be able to recognize and even draw it into your life outside of that class. Another option, if you're so inclined, is to go take a seat at a 12–Step meeting where you will not be expected to show up other than as yourself. The connection that blossoms and comes forth in these rooms where I am not judged for being unique in my ways amongst others who are not judged for being unique in their ways is the greatest gift of spirituality I've ever given myself. There, I am not dependent on anyone but my Higher Power and neither is anybody else. Within that self–governance, we are bound and connected. There, we elevate the authenticity we each come in with and how everything that comes with it—how it's courageous, how it can be challenging, how we are each irreplaceable and matchless—is what binds us to one another. We choose to connect from different brains and personalities to different brains and personalities in the spirit of a shared experience, like birds who fly together.

Question for You

Last week, I was taking an outdoor cycling class, and the instructor kept telling us to listen to the beat and to do our best to stay on the same foot as one another. The instructor wasn't so much interested in the choreography of what we were doing but in reminding us that when we ride together as a union, we are so much stronger than when we choose to ride alone. I know this book is meant to be somewhat spiritual and thinking–based, but for the action in this conversation, I'd like to encourage you to exercise with a group this week. There is something about melding with the exertion and fun of others as you move your body to whatever extent you can that gives energy. It's what we lack when we work out alone – the combined magic of moving our own body (autonomy) and doing it together (connection).

Note we don't copy how someone else moves (dependence). This is a physical experience, but also mental and spiritual. We are independent and celebrating that independence with other independent beings. Nobody moves in the exact same way, nobody's fingerprints are the same, nobody's DNA, and yet we all have moves, prints, and genes... so we're the same but different.

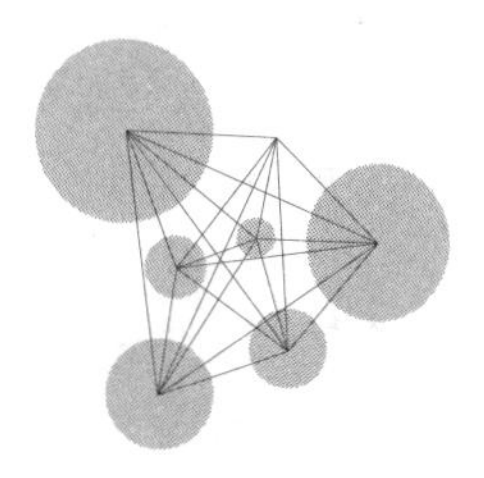

Conversation Seventeen: From Anxiety to Movement

In my life, I have often felt shame around grief. A friend lost his dog and was absolutely beside himself, bedridden with sadness for days. My initial reaction was to sit in judgment. How can someone be so sad over losing an animal? Then I thought to myself: Who am I to judge how someone grieves? Who am I to judge the way one processes their pain? I turned inward and found there are no prescriptions or right ways when grieving.

When my father passed away, I was saddened but not overly so, and I judged myself for not being sadder. Several months later, out of nowhere, a deep sadness befell me, and at first, I wasn't sure what it was or where it came from. I felt it take over my body. As I analyzed my feelings more carefully, I realized it was the grief over losing my father. I so badly wanted him to come in a dream to somehow communicate with me, to confirm me, to give me his guidance. In addition to grieving the loss of my father, I also grieved for the relationship I wanted to have with him, mourning the wish I held for decades to have been understood by him. The sorrow engulfed me and created new reasons to be melancholy about his death.

This resulted in a huge amount of anxiety I carried around. What helped me move through it was moving my body. Movement allowed me time and space, a place to put my pain, a sense of patience for the grief, and the acknowledgment that no two episodes of grieving need look alike like no two dance moves need to look alike. The body is stable, and it is in flux. Movement creates room. Anxiety is rigid, tight and suffocating. I have suffered from anxiety for most of my life, which has been both a blessing and a curse. It's a blessing because anxiety motivates me and gets me going. It's a curse because it gives me a skewed perspective of life and of self. It brings my defenses up and down. The ultimate negative is when I buy into the message and tell myself that I don't belong in whatever group I seek to be part of. There, I label myself an outsider, and I disconnect because nobody cares if I am there or not. In that mindset, I don't even want to move.

A teacher taught me that our feelings, emotions, and actions attempt to protect us and make us feel safe when usually they do the exact opposite. Case in point: I'm part of a men's group that meets quarterly, and I always leave early. I'd never known about this until it was pointed out to me a few weeks ago. The truth is, I adore these men and all I want is to be part of their circle, yet unknowingly, I had been leaving early so they wouldn't ever abandon me or hurt me. By leaving early, I was abandoning them. The thing was that by avoiding deeper connection, I was hurting myself. I remain so grateful that my men's group brought this up to me and that I had the courage to walk through my discomfort and fear instead of running away for good. I faced my anxiety, took the unconscious and made it conscious, thus understanding for myself what I was actually doing and how I was moving – literally and figuratively – away from my goal of belonging instead of moving towards it. Sometimes, the movement is a thought process or a leaving. It's hard to face our negative messaging and dig deeper to get a better understanding of ourselves.

We can align with movement, no matter our conditions or circumstances. I visited my friend Rabbi Yitzy who is paralyzed in his body. The first thing he asked me was how my son Nate is doing. I haven't seen the Rabbi in a month, and he's only met my son once, yet he remembered who he was. The identification from him of my son—my active, moving, healthy son—meant so much to us! Though the Rabbi can only control eye movement, which is how he communicates, his mind is intact. At the same time, he remains a prisoner in his body. I asked him, "Rabbi, how do you deal with sadness on the days that are painful? How do you deal with grieving the life you used to live?"

He told me he does three things: 1.) He helps others, showing them how even a prisoner has the choice of movement with his eyes and with his attitude. 2.) He watches comedic movies, which is a source of laughter for him. And what is laughter but a surge of emotion flowing through the body? Laughter is positivity in motion, generated by one and appreciated by another. Laughter moves between us and generates connection, which makes it a connecting expression, and 3.) The Rabbi listens to music. Music is vibration. Music is kinetic. Music is a crusade of sound waves. The Rabbi's humanity and especially his love for life made me smile from ear to ear, as he lived vicariously through my son, as he let himself be carried by giggles and songs and service. He was not stagnant but very much traveling life in these ways. We ended our visit by setting a date for my next visit, where I promised to bring my son Nate with me so we could watch Ferris Bueller's Day Off together the three of us.

I tell you this story because Rabbi Yitzy has every reason to sink into a soup of anxiety, depression, and despair. He is unwell physically and limited by it. Yet still, he finds the movement of life, the ride of breath in and breath out. It is so nice to look up to heroes and people of greatness. It makes me realize that connection achieves greatness. Him not getting a medal or an award, just sitting talking with me, remembering my son, that's greatness. Movement is available to us, inside of us. It connects our bones and organs, our neurons and synapses and cells, it is our energy doing what it is meant to do. It also connects us as a tactic to overcome sadness. Life throws us curveballs, and no one escapes without them; yet the tools that we use to make suffering meaningful and tolerable use our pain as a point for others when they meet their pain, and so it moves from me to you, you to me.

Life isn't only about pursuing happiness, which can be fleeting, but about pursuing movement, which is a form of happiness in pure form because movement directs our energy into a response, reply, reaction, and expression. It is somatically healing to move. It happens not only in our heads but in our whole bodies as an extension of our minds. It is our beings moving through the body, the glorious body that works for us and that we get to work. Go to a dance recital, and I dare you not to feel connected. Go to a ballroom and watch people waltz, and I dare you not to notice your body tingling. It's why Rabbi Yitzy is powerless, and he can still move. He has found healthy ways to continue connecting so he can help others find meaning and celebrate the connection between bodies.

Depression, addiction, compulsions, anxiety—these are not questions of willpower, unwillingness to be happy, selfishness or something wrong with a person. As an addict myself, I know firsthand what it is to wish my mind didn't share self–defeating stories with me. I wished for years I wasn't anxious and felt mostly shame for the way I was. It was the greatest factor in continuing my disconnection and the greatest barrier to getting help. Loving someone as they are is not condoning them. It is saying you provide the space for them to move into their best selves and heal themselves when they're ready to do so, and it is holding that space. It is holding connection for them when they cannot hold it. It is holding the room to dance in the future.

Be a ballet studio – you as a human. Be a room with white walls, with bars, with music, with twirling, with windows, with a stereo, with mirrors. Be a space for others to come into and feel seen and heard, to bow and plie and pirouette. You have no idea what an impact that can make in someone's life – not to give them more reasons to be anxious and hate themselves but to provide the opportunity for them to move through it with you holding the light for them as they find their way towards a harmony they can dance to. This will give them the chance to connect to themselves through the gracious joy of movement.

Question for You

As Rumi says in his poem The Guest House, when he mentions depression and sorrow, pain and shame, "Welcome and entertain them all!" Even negative emotions bring gifts, and we must include them all as real parts of the human experience. If we face all of our internal messages, no matter how dark they are, we get vulnerable enough to share our fears and understand our actions. From this place of intimate connection with all parts of ourselves, we can move towards meeting our true goals that lead us to connect with others.

I'd like you to pause, close your eyes, and find your breath. Feel into your body. Ask yourself what you might be grieving right now—a person, a relationship, a pet, a dream, a job, an idea, an opportunity, a country. And I'd like you to assess how you are processing your grief, if you are processing it, and what it might feel like to stand up from this place of awareness and move it in your body. Whether it be going for a walk, taking a yoga class, or going to a nightclub, move with the energetic currents of grief to make peace within yourself. No blocks, no resistance. Move from this place of peace, and there will be a connection to whatever you are mourning. In that connection, the person, place, thing or idea never dies.

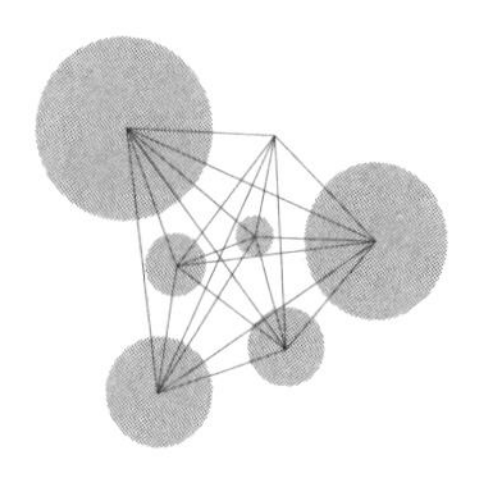

Conversation Eighteen: From Anger To Creativity

All that energy and fire we generate when we are angry can be used to make something. And in that sacred action of turning our fury into creativity, we connect with others in one of the most raw and holy ways. Recently, I was reading the words of Rabbi Jonathan Sacks as he spoke of hate and racism: "I asked Judea Pearl, father of the murdered journalist David Pearl, why he was working for reconciliation between Jews and Muslims. He replied with heartbreaking lucidity, 'Hate killed my son. Therefore, I am determined to fight hate.'" Sacks was referring to how people can convert fury into vision, and how to do that, we have to strive to come to and come through the emotion of anger.

We have all been trained to view someone different than us as other. Our brains make up a story about them depending on how they look, and we determine in an instant if they are safe or unsafe, scary or kind. It is not intentional. It is not natural; it is a system we've built as humans to stand on implicit biases so ingrained in our collective psyches they feel as if they are part of our DNA. These biases act like facts. But they're not—they are neither organic to who we are nor the truth. These assessments are prejudiced, not reflective of who other people actually are, but only of what we've learned or unlearned. It is easy to be mad about this—mad at the world, at society, at the human brain, at our families, at those who other us, even at those we other. And I'm here to say that your wrath is okay because only from that honest starting line can we make our way to inspiration, to seeing others and the world through connection.

Think of times when we have invested in in rage, in disconnection. Think of situations where we lacked an adequate stage to healthily process our anger so it can be coped with and then used to create peace. If we don't know how to do this inside ourselves individually when we're triggered, how can we expect to enact this collectively on a national or global level, people to people? It has to be okay, it has to be safe to feel so we can get to what lies beyond the anger which is even more important: coexistence. We must listen to one another, come together, and get resourceful so everybody can live well. We must be allowed to connect to our anger to access deeper creativity, and then we can connect to others' anger and build the world we want to see together. We need to elevate connection so that it's not only popular but infectious. Because only connection will save us. Not a particular political party or a governmental position, but all of us deciding collectively that collaboration must be fought for, designed, and cooler than staying in rage and shock, hate and fear.

I am not perfect at this. Sometimes, my resentments resurface and I don't want to let go. Steeped in unawareness to the fact that I'm doing this, I cut off a road for others to connect to me. It's not just those I'm mad at, it's the pathway that gets shut down, closing me off to them, but also to everyone else, like a highway exit that's not open, not just to your car but to all cars. It becomes unusable, inaccessible. The thing is, creativity is the antithesis to the block. I know this, and you know this, but we forget it when fury blinds us. It's a heavy burden to carry, walking around enraged, and we need connection with other people to remind us of what we already know, which is that processing resentments lets us move on and generate something meaningful. Learning how to be with the fire within can actually be a freeing tool of connection so that instead of forever blazing and fanning flames, we can make something new from the tender soil of burnt ash. They say that after a fire, the land is more fertile, that it can grow lusher and more beautiful crops. So it must be true for the landscape of your soul where connection can be the soil itself.

On a closer note, I had the privilege of going to Israel with my sister so we could help our mom move into a retirement community. The experience was wonderful, and the camaraderie with my sister made me feel close to her. It also made regret how much time we do not share in each other's company. It made me think a lot about love and how love can feel like an obligation, a duty, a responsibility chained around our necks that we cannot break free from. I want to state this because this idea of love causes separation, not connection. It paves the way for more anger, not creativity. Love need not be earned over time; it's earned biologically once we are born and here. It isn't conditional on liking one's behavior, it is unconditional because we are all creations of something more, and we can love people without liking their behavior. We can be mad and still be loving.

I'm blessed to like my children and I'm lucky that I get to be proud of them too. The truth is I'd love them no matter what. Unconditional love is loving a person even when they're not behaving the way we want them to, even if they're objectionable, and by that, I don't mean be a doormat, I mean boundaries should be implemented, but boundary–making and setting is a creative endeavor! It's your disappointment in others that fuels your anger; it is okay to welcome the feeling and expression of that anger so you can arrive at a creative space of connection. It is not only true for the world but for the circle of our own families and our personal relationships. Being mad at someone does not have to eclipse love. Nothing shall. Saying no, managing a firm yet gentle approach to healthy boundaries, setting examples and leading by living them, these approaches bypass consequences and punishment, threats and bribes, and keep the connection alive even if you do not agree or condone them. You can let the anger go. This will more than likely make sure our loved ones will behave in a way that we don't mind as much—because of our love, not because we threaten to take it away. Acting out of unprocessed anger is selfish. Taking out our frustrations on our children or loved ones is selfish. Using connection as a tool, as a weapon, to get what we want at the expense of what someone else wants is selfish.

There is an auspicious day in the Jewish Calendar called Lag Baomer. It's the day the students of the great sage Rabbi Akiva stopped dying. To understand the significance, let's understand why they were dying and why we celebrate by first going over a brief history of who Rabbi Akiva was. Rabbi Akiva was illiterate until he was 40 years old when he saw water penetrate a rock and said to himself, "If water can penetrate a rock, so can knowledge penetrate my brain." He then studied, amassing 14,000 students who perished because they did not treat each other respectfully or kindly. They regarded one another out of jealousy and anger, which unprocessed and with nowhere to go, led to their death. With only four remaining students, Rabbi Akiva wrote the entire Talmud. We celebrate Lag Baomer because we celebrate persistence and the creativity required for that persistence to be possible. We celebrate Lag Baomer because we believe in righteous anger, but moreover in the innovation and connection born out of it. Five people can be left after all that rage to connect and write a book with the potential to help change the world.

We can do that...together.

Question for You

We don't talk enough about what to do with mad. About how mad can be connective tissue and how mad is simply energy burning, which we can use to make something. What if we instead allowed anger, let it blaze, and let it be natural so it can move through us and turn into power? What if we shed light on what we do – and were truthful about it and held it with open eyes and fanned the flames? What if we allowed ourselves to question our assumptions and to imagine other meanings that can be more accurate about who people are? What if we understood that everybody can do all of this and there is potential to connect with everyone?

There is no other way to effectively combat biases. As a Jewish man who wishes for people to do this when they see me, trust me when I say, it's one of the most important things we can do. So how can I get it for myself? By giving it to others. By investigating my prejudice, continuing to face it and rage against it, to rage with it, and then take that energy to create something better. I ask of you now to summon up the courage to look at your misconceptions and to let all the feelings come up and out for you to return to your original nature as a soul who only invents reasons to connect repeatedly. Flow with fury and let it propel you towards passion.

PART THREE

WHAT YOU SAY

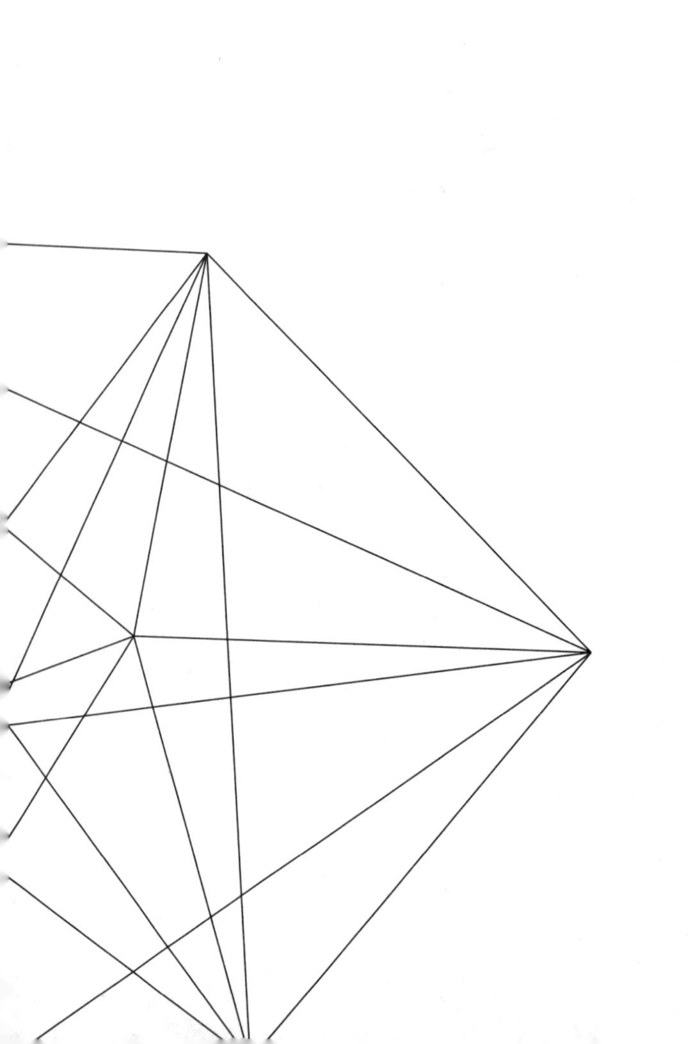

We've sat with what we believe and what we do. Now let's dive into what we say. Our words, the rivers that flow from our mouths with the potential to nourish, flood, or dry out the grounds of our existence.

I have often wished that through thinking alone I could change my life. Nobody would have to watch me flail, or reach, or miss. That means nobody can know me, because I wouldn't have to be vulnerable or humble, or worse, humiliated, at least not in front of others. Vulnerability means something different for every person. It is not a universal definition, or a one size fits all model. For me, I have no hiccups about sharing my recovery or being a clown for others. My vulnerability comes from asking for help. "Help me," I struggle to say. It requires upmost effort for me to let myself be supported, and it's how I have identified what vulnerability means: it means the place where we take off our masks. It is admitting we were wrong, it is admitting we can't do this thing alone, it is the thing we are protecting ourselves from saying out loud, from owning, from confessing.

So I want to ask you now to think about what your vulnerability might be, the place where your façade crumbles and you feel most naked. Because there is no other way to become the you, you want to be, the you, you want to feel like you're allowed to be, other than by facing the answer to that question. Leaning right into it.

This is how we begin to be who we are out loud. Inside out, outside in, all of you matters, in full color, whether singing or shouting or whispering, but in every way speaking yourself into reality, especially where the trashing comes to life. We need to experience all of ourselves to be known and for our connections to be real.

Once upon a time, I thought I knew everything. I did. I believed my thoughts were right and that my actions were righteous and that my words were to be heeded. I need you to know so that as you read onwards you hear an honest tone in my voice and not one of judgment. What I off here is camaraderie. I've been where you are. I'm still there as I begin anew each day. And you are already going where you're going. You're already a higher version of you than you were before you began this book. So imagine my words as if they are written on a poster board beside you, and you're a runner in a marathon. I am cheering you on. Your pace, your timing, your stride, your imperfect journey, you are doing it. I am screaming your name as you take the greatest, most miraculous action ever: you live. You move through life.

It is an honor to be heard. We know deep within ourselves whether we are pouring out constants and vowels that bind us or syllables intended to destroy ourselves and others. Our words say so much more about how we feel inside, about what it feels like for us to look at ourselves the mirror, than they will ever say about anyone else. Our words might affect others, but they absolutely affect us as they reflect our inner monologues and the standards in which we allow ourselves to be spoken to by ourselves.

Words can be prayers. Words can be songs. Words can build poems. Words can lift others up. Words can teach. What we say can result in more connection and beauty and wholeness. Why would we waste that opportunity when through words alone—through writing what we wish to speak or telling it to someone while looking straight into their eyes or passing on stories to a group at a campfire—we have the potential to reach communion?

Did you know that sound waves are used in medicine? Or that sound waves can be used to create art? Sound is used in SONAR to find the depth of the sea. Think of how important what we say is–it is made from a collision of molecules, leaving whoever it reaches affected and changed. What we say penetrates! Vibrations make sound waves that move through materials and leave that matter shaken, shifted or transformed, from particle to particle. Put succinctly: what we say has the power to change lives. So, let's speak wisely. And when it's somebody else's turn to talk, maybe grant them the greatest blessing and let their sound hit you and move you, let it connect you to them even if you agree with them or not. Let us listen.

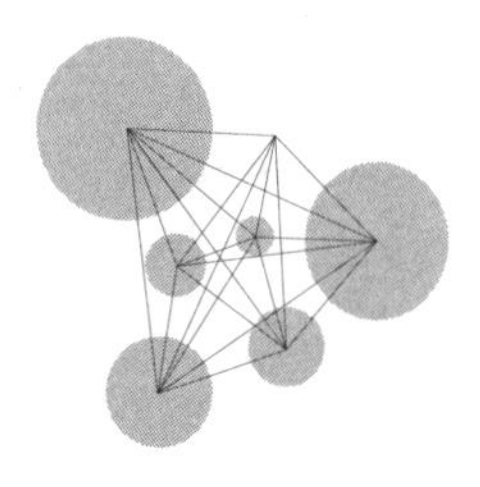

Conversation Nineteen: From Hurt To Healed

Impatience and anxiety remove us from our ability to see the positive messages right in front of our eyes. Then, we often have the audacity to talk about how unloved we are by others, by God, by life. When we do this, the words we utter sentence us to more time disconnected. When we do this, we speak only more hurt into existence.

Recently, I was at a religious observance where an older rabbi had to blow the shofar (a ram's horn) 110 times. At around the 65th blast, the guy was exhausted. I thought he was finished as he stood unable to catch his breath, hunched over. The rabbi kept going, slowly, methodically, one more puff at a time. Meanwhile, I was crawling out of my skin. I felt like I couldn't wait for it to be over or for somebody to tap him out. That's how uncomfortable I was watching him struggle to force sound from the horn. Then I began to mumble about it to the people around me, to whisper, to mime and to share my sentiments. And it was only after I'd spoken my complaints that the sounds of the shofar came in to override my own words. What was left afterwards, in the silence of my mouth and from my mouth, was my discomfort, not as something to impart on others, unintentionally asking them to carry it with me. But for me to sit with. For me to tolerate alone. There I was, noticing my enormous impatience, my anxiety, my desire and ability to so easily hang onto a *woe is me* storyline that reflects some hardship I am enduring that I need somebody else to bear along with me.

When the silence comes in after that awareness, if we're listening to ourselves and if we have a spirituality, no matter what kind it is, underneath the resistance will be a sense of awe. Only when I saw outside of what I said could the awe descend on me.

Awe at the rabbi's perseverance barreled into me. Awe at how much time the rabbi gave me to be in a house of worship and in community because of how long he took to do the job. Awe at the chance to sit in my squirming skin and be with it so I could build my love muscles and connect to what was going on.

My next instinct was to feel ashamed. I'd expressed my desire to rush and shush a fellow rabbi! Then I realized the moment had brought me great healing, a chance to love myself despite my imperfections, and a chance to use any touchstone of hurt as an opening to heal. It had to be this way because healing takes patience, and I hadn't been listening. Healing requires that we stick around long enough for the slow process to move us through its pace. Healing takes anxiety because it brings up discomfort, and only once we can hold space for our anxieties can we have the strength to heal them. Then, the most magical thing will happen if we experience this: because we get to do it for ourselves, we will get to see it for others. It will tie us further to our community because we will need our people in our moments of wobbliness, and they will need us. Hurt to healing breeds connection. I waited until the 110th shofar blow was over and the rabbi was done. Then, I used my voice differently. "What a great job he did," I declared to the people around me, the same ones I'd spoken to before. I hoped to even out the negative ions I'd formed in the room prior with this new perspective.

This is the reason we need people to support us when it's harder, when the potholes cause accidents, for the delays we must endure when we need to rest. For when we need to practice the most important word, many of us will cringe as we learn how to say, *Help*. Having safe people in your life means not only the chance for deep connection, and that you can be vulnerable and accountable enough to heal with them. To have others who believe in you even when you slip and don't believe in yourself is a gamechanger. And it means you reflect safety and support equally back to them when they slip too.

To be able to speak power to healing over hurting, I want to gently nudge you to establish accountability partners and say your rawness to them and receive theirs in return. If you have no idea where to start this, consider a 12–Step program. There are many Al–Anon meetings open to the public, and realistically speaking, who wouldn't benefit from a group of people talking about issues with control and codependency? Accountability is an essential part of connection and healing, and 12–Step programs do accountability well. Don't worry about if what you say is interesting or if someone will laugh at you (these are codependent patterns that keep us designed to focus on others and not ourselves); just start putting yourself out there and trust that because we can't control other people's responses, whatever we get back is part of the opportunity for more healing. However small, in however few words you need to speak your vulnerabilities. Ask even one person or a few someones or share at a meeting; discuss your feelings, the ups and the downs and the progress.

In the program, we find a "sponsor," and the others in the room become our "fellows." You don't necessarily have to qualify in extreme or obvious ways in order to join a meeting. There are more online meetings now than ever, so it is always possible to find a circle to sit in and say what needs to be heard, as well as to hear what needs to be connected to. As we say when we share, spend one minute on the problem (the hurt, how things used to be) and two minutes on the solution (the healing.) This is a good rule of thumb in life, I believe. There are various other options to consider too, such as counseling and therapy services both locally or online, or going to talk to members of a clergy you feel aligned with, or even calling a sibling to share what's going on for you.

When we create space for other people to connect with us, when we speak our need for support, a mode of connection that is so small yet so huge, we will discover that isolation is an option, not a decree. We can go out and meet people who understand, we can have conversations and commonalities and find a person to talk to. And when we introduce those people to each other, connections will be amplified. We not only change our world in this way, but we also change others' worlds. This is how we make community, one loving and lovely. You can even extrapolate from the 12–Step program without having to actually join a 12–Step program if you don't want to. Create your own "sponsor" and "fellows" if the program isn't for you, through your community, your neighborhood, and your friends.

Regardless, I implore you to build your circle based on the sincerity that lives inside you, as it lives inside each of us. As our hurt loses its hold, not only in our minds and thoughts and then in our actions but also in the confirmations we preach when we speak about ourselves, we connect and reconnect in ways truly healing. The more we speak our stories, the more we hear other stories, the more we realize it is one story. There is nothing better than a circle of surrender. We begin to reveal. We expose our souls. And this will be a call out for others who do the same.

Question for You

Is there an area where you are speaking into the hurt instead of moving through it to get to the healing? I don't mean rush through it, for to connect to ourselves genuinely we must feel all feelings, even the negative feelings. Especially the negative feelings. But this does not involve sharing our negativity again and again on repeat with anybody nearby, and in doing so, giving ourselves temporary relief, like letting a little steam out of a pipe. At some point, we strive to see that we are circling a drain. We are a race car on the same loop instead of taking the exit ramp for some other city, some new adventure of being with our hurt, feeling it through, and then moving into healing.

Think about a speech you give again and again, a story you retell as truth. As you consider other perspectives about this story, look at what is underneath it or around it and look at the neglected angles to find opportunities for healing. Plan for bumps along the road, and perhaps consider having that accountability group we've mentioned ready for you to sink into when it gets hard to move through the hurt. You will though. What waits on the other side is the feeling of repair within yourself.

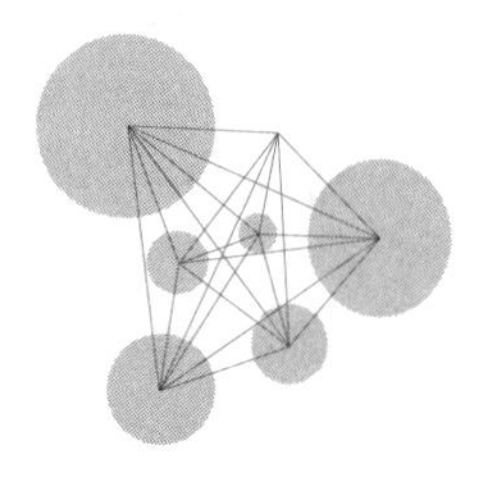

Conversation Twenty: From Problem To Solution

As you let go of the memorized scripts of hurt, as you trend yourself toward healing, you will begin to build the bridge from who you were to who you will be, one plank of decency at a time. And you will cross the abyss of your problems and fears, addictions, and disorders and walk straight into living the solutions you seek.

Because of the community you have assembled through how you speak and the people you attract who also speak the same language, you will create a life around being the person you've always wanted to be. Connection makes us feel better about ourselves. Because of what I think, what I say, and what I do, these stems merge into a new bouquet, and I can shift my life and what it's made up of. Not drama, but delight. Not chaos, but clarity. Not problems, but solutions. When I am living in connection, what's going on in the social media lands or anywhere else I am not standing or sitting in with my body is way less significant than being in the great flow of real life, looking for reasons to love the life I've already got, the one I am in right now, offscreen when nobody is watching. Love and abundance come when we finally realize all we need to do is FIND the love and abundance in the moments we're in. One minute at a time. We search for it. We see it. We hold it up with glee. It's already here; it's already ours. We exclaim about it. This is how we create more of it. THIS IS GOOD. I AM GOOD. RIGHT NOW. (Yes, all caps.)

Not to oversimplify, but this way of thinking can solve every problem.

When our reality stops being an addiction to finding difficulty and starts being a scavenger hunt for joy, we give ourselves (and everyone around us) an enormous boost. And if when we make a mistake and submerge back into our crises–mode again (we are human after all), we have to get back up so we can return to enjoying this amazing ride we're on of being alive. Picking a new lens through which we see the world, tinting our beliefs with a new color, is the most important process we will ever undergo. Through the spoken word, we can seal this shift. We can paint it into being, from thought to form.

The chance to find solutions and leave a positive residue on everything we feel is how we connect not only within ourselves but with others, as well as with every atom and cell on this planet. Because that we're here means we can solve problems. That's what aliveness can do. So even after we mess up, slide back into tired programs, or the *everything is crappy* word tornado strikes again, when all we talk about is how it's all turned gray, we are aware now! We can choose a new filter anytime we want and spin a new tale.

Sometimes, it's inside out (thoughts to the external). I've found sometimes it's outside in (my words influence my thoughts). And we will wake up again, and next time not be asleep for as long, until one day, solution thinking becomes our resting state. Being solution–oriented is a connection state of being. It's up to each of us to choose, on our own time and in our way, although the ache and the old patterns might still exist and feel intoxicating when they visit us, to meet negativity, hug it, cradle it, sing it a lullaby...and then let it go. When we listen to and love our problems for all their nastiness, we align with our higher selves. Then, we can speak the words that chase negativity away. There will be nothing left after that other than positivity. One moment at a time, we get all these chances to keep choosing solutions. We are that lucky every day, every minute, to let life be just that.

We are wired for this connection. With ourselves and one another, with God, with the force that embraces us each day we open our eyes. We must share out loud the connection we feel to pass it on and change this world, to make positivity cooler than complaining. We must connect to live and live to connect.

I've seen how connection can restore a human to wholeness no matter what they've experienced. Engaging and participating can do that to a person. Conversations back and forth can do that to a person. Living as a solution because living IS the solution that can do that to a person. That's why language matters so very much. The fabric stitches cultures and countries together.

The invisible moments where we reach beyond ourselves and connect within ourselves a breath at the same time is when we link up to the magic. Inside to go out. Outside brings us back in. Wellness cannot come from seeking the reasons the disconnection exists in the first place; it cannot come from focusing on what is wrong, and it cannot come from someone else or something else. Not when we're eight years old and not as an adult. Because if connection is given to us by someone else, it can be taken away, and then we never had it. No, connection is a spark born from and feeds on itself. Living to find reasons to connect is a lifestyle choice that brings good feelings and good speaking. Now, I want to repeat that I'm not talking about Pollyanna positive thinking, where you lie to yourself or trick yourself or force manifestation. Doubt and shame are our biggest adversaries, and part of this work is to learn how to sit with problems, acknowledge and hear them, value their input and not deny their existence, but also not be controlled by them. Solutions will not always mean cures or guarantees, and they don't always turn out rosy. We can look at them as points of connection that are the wisest and best options for us and choose to feel taken care of by the Universe. We can see solutions and positivity and love in our current life, now as it is, until BAM! What starts as a small trickling becomes a geyser. Solution–oriented, problem–solving, positive people. Like anchors in the ocean that reach into the ground. We become people so magnificently natural to connect with because it flows from our mouths because it's what we hear rushing into our ears. It becomes who we are.

Last thing I'll say here: to usher in more connection, to bring ourselves to safety, to healing, to honesty, to love, we must accept there is no one–time fix. This will not be a box we check. The answers we seek are fluid. Because the problems may keep changing and keep coming. This requires our consistent responsiveness, flexibility, and soft handling. The solutions we will focus on where there used to be problems might change yearly, sometimes daily. We don't need to spend as much time, energy, or money trying to fix things because there is no fix to disconnection. There is only us sharing what our soul calls for when it calls for it so we can stop living in problems, constraints, burdens and grievances. There is more to life than this.

Question for You

In the program of recovery there is a saying: you are only as sick as your secrets.

To connect, I suggest speaking a secret out loud even if just to one other person, even if it's a stranger. You never know when the thing you say will touch another person at the exact moment they need it. And as you share, as you reveal yourself and get through the process, check in with yourself after. I invite you not to overlook the temptation to be done with it and instead circle back with yourself later and assess: Do you feel relieved that you allowed yourself to be seen?

You're allowed to say no. It is probably worth noting.

Adjust accordingly and without apology when it does not feel good to you, for you. We must keep wondering what we can do or say or think to get back to what is already in us, with us, and of us. The mission comes from you because the mission *is* you. We know it's one day at a time. We may not realize it is one second at a time. That is to say, YOU are one second at a time, and so is connection. Commit to fanning its flame within your scope of expression. Often, magic is created between two beings, similarly to how neurons communicate energy through the synapse, through the gaps between them. Trust in solutions that can organically come from the jump off of you and onto another. That is the energy of problems morphing beyond themselves.

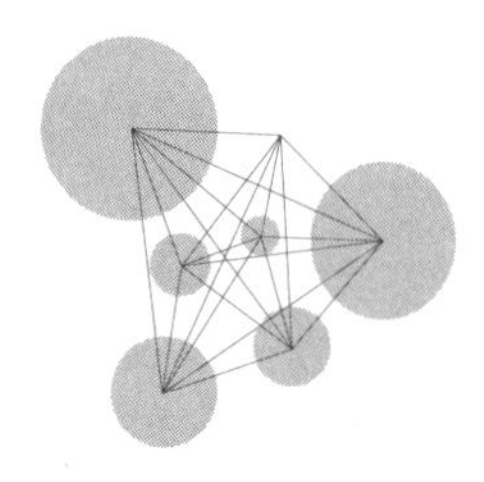

Conversation Twenty–One: From Stress To Stillness

We all have stress in our lives. Some of us have more stress than others, and some of us cling to our stress more than others, but what we get when we continue to live addicted to stress, pressure, and tension is a sense of brokenness, a complete fear that life sucks. It causes distraction, anger, and scarcity to reign supreme politically, religiously, nationally, and spiritually. From here, it's all too easy to tell ourselves it's somebody else's fault to face the bad bet we made on somebody else over ourselves by letting our lives be dictated by the idea that we are never enough. The trap is then in thinking no stress is the way to be. That is not only impossible, it also doesn't work, as we need a little tension to keep the friction of resistance that causes movement forward. So the remedy for stress we prescribe is rarely a remedy but a pipe dream, an illusion that leads to more comparison between us and more stress.

A compare and despair attitude has been the foundation for the virtual world we now spend hours upon hours in, hiding behind our crafted poses and our smiles and our manipulations and our illusions with a filter, hoping we can act our way into feeling like we are okay. This life isn't what we were made for – doing it somebody else's way, pretending, unnatural, manmade, and blaming somebody for having more than us, while somebody blames us because they have less. If social media did breed connection, wouldn't it have made us the most content, enlightened people ever by now? If social media worked to foster true friendships, wouldn't we have stopped needing to buy things or amass things or eat things or shatter things by now? Social media is capitalism on steroids. It's meant to keep us apart from God, our true selves, and the truth, which is we are all one.

We know this; we know that the online semblance of satisfaction is not true satisfaction, we can look up millions of articles on Google about how the Internet and technology have isolated us more than any other advancement in human history. It knowing only takes us halfway there. Knowledge dangles us above the awareness of the chasm we feel inside, which often feels like it has no words to adequately express itself. Wisdom points out that we may have fallen, and from that vantage point, we might see all of the destruction, but it does not lead us to build ourselves back up. That doesn't come from knowing but from unknowing. It actually doesn't come from what we say, either. It comes from what we do *not* say.

The inability to turn off my mind, disconnect from my electronics, and escape my anxiety prevents me from being and makes it difficult for me to enjoy any experience. Meditation has helped me recover from stress by helping me do nothing other than return to my commitment to stay present. I won't kid you; I'm not good at sitting still with my eyes closed. The point is I do it anyway. The point is I feel what I fear missing out on by turning off for a while and then I survive the missing out and prove to myself that I can. Sometimes, meditations go great, and they bring me so much peace and insight. Other times I struggle not to think, not to squirm, I stay there and stick to it. That's all that is required of me to access what happens when I stop moving and thinking and distracting myself and lying drowned in my subconscious program, believing the noise as real life. Trust me, it is a frigging gift to meditate and stop the record for a while. I cannot recommend it enough, even though I know you're rolling your eyes as you read this because you've heard "go meditate" a hundred times before. Seriously, the antidote for stress is sitting under a tree and doing only breathing. It is the opposite of everything being pushed in our faces.

I had a meeting with a prominent businessperson recently and couldn't believe he had a flip phone with no Internet access. I asked him why he didn't have a Smartphone, to which he replied that he could not focus on any task at hand, and on his life happening all around him. He felt it rude to be with his family and then stop to tend to somebody's text who was not even in his house, ignoring the people in front of him who love him! He felt it rude to abandon his work or his passion to tend to an email. The thought of getting rid of my Smartphone caused me to panic as he told me this, he inspired me to take contrary action and start to give myself regular electronic breaks. Mini technology vacations. Now I understand him. I get how it is nonsensical to believe that it would be more connecting to disconnect from what is in my present situation so I can instead be in the land of make–believe and communicate through air transmission! What have we done to the threads of community?

Perhaps nothing is more obviously ruined than politics in today's climate. Instead of working with the other party, instead of being part of the solution and holding space for the beauty that exists in our views and differences, we blame and tear down and stay siloed and refuse to collaborate. We use tools made for connection to sever ourselves from one another, learning to identify way more with what we do not like than what we do like, therefore fixating on the issues rather than proactively seeking unifiers. We won't listen. We won't compromise. And because of this, we aren't serving the citizens or the country. However, if we could only stop the stress and strain. If our governments could only model for the people how to be still, how to work together, how to build bridges, how to lead. Why aren't our officials meditating and going still, why aren't they recognizing connection as a daily choice they must make within themselves and outside of themselves?

Social media is as much of a drug as any other drug. It was designed to work that way on purpose. To get you outside of yourself, searching for somebody to be wrong, especially you. Social media makes us cowardly because with it, we don't have to be in life, other than to post something for likes, which is not what we came here for. This fake connection, fake joy, fake relief, fake away–ness, fake highs, it will not do. It will not fill us. It all just leads us to want more of the fakeness that gave us the taste of what we can feel and who we can be if we turned off, turned away from everything fake, anything else other than what is inside of us, which is the only real thing in the world, and offered it to ourselves in the present. Then, and only then, can we align with our true voice and be the heroes of our own stories by staying loyal to that inside light we are. Then, we can invite those we wish to near the borders of our hearts.

Question for You

Jewish tradition commands us to shut off our phones and all electronics on the Sabbath, which is one of my favorite customs of this faith. If we don't set aside time to be in the here and now, quiet and tapping into tranquility, how can we expect to know what connection is? Every Shabbat, I walk instead of drive, I sit with my family by a fire instead of reading another news article online, and I slow way down. So now I turn it over to you. I invite you to set aside five minutes, maybe ten, and meditate. Yes, really. With this book before you, it's as if you're not alone. I am there. You might play a guided meditation, you might play music, maybe you will sit in absolute silence, but be still and be with your breath, and that's it. You don't need to go to a fancy retreat to learn how. You don't need to make it a big deal. You need to shut your eyes and breathe. To just begin. This is a tiny timeout in an otherwise busy life, and it requires no words at all from you.

Here's a second exercise for you to do, perhaps after you meditate. Have a meaningful discussion or discourse with someone you often disagree with *after* you've meditated, especially if you don't see eye to eye with them politically. And see what happens, how you speak, how you listen, how you understand one another, at least from your end. Test this; the proof is in the pudding. I predict you will begin to actually see where this other person is coming from, without the need to get defensive and without the need to attack. Wouldn't all sides benefit from this since healthy communication leads to growth, harmony and inclusivity? Isn't this the way to construe connection, one mindful still breath at a time that expands instead of constricts? Because here is the thing about meditation: you can become addicted to it. And as an addict myself, I'll shock you and say it's the only addiction I will allow myself. Meditation is more than just about sitting down with my eyes closed; is a way to live. Washing dishes, tucking my grandchild into bed, walking down the street, writing to you—all of it is meditation if I am still enough inside and present enough outside with you.

Thanks to this way of life, I don't need my phone much, other than when I want to make phone calls or for emergencies. Because I'm dedicated to connecting, I'm dedicated to the stillness required to reach it. Put down your iPhone and join me, won't you?

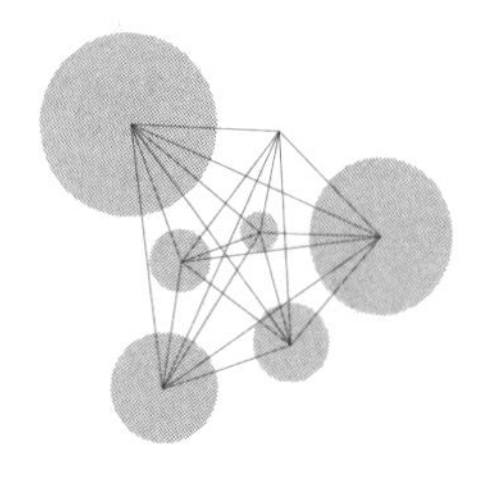

Conversation Twenty–Two: From Complaining to Content

How often do we say this to ourselves: "If only this, then that." If only I were richer, smarter, prettier, fill in the blanker, then my life would be so much easier, better, happier, fill in the blanker. Too often, I think that if I only had more [insert a long list here for me], then I wouldn't struggle with any of my greatest ills—addiction, depression, self–doubt, or management of my finances.

Intellectually, I know this to be a false statement, but the weight of my insecurities and self–pity can sometimes create a blocker. This blocker costs me in connection, mostly because it turns me into a mega whiner. You might call that a fault–finding mentality. I lose sight of that which drives me forward, that which reminds me of how fortunate and blessed I truly am, and it possesses me with soliloquies of complaint. I recently read an article that reminded me of the power of perspective. While it seems trivial, the article called out how people with large jets often make fun of people with smaller jets. How ridiculous is that? I realized no matter how much we accumulate, humans have a terrible tendency to rely on the outside to give us a sense of worth. The value of our lives must come from inside, from a choice to be content as we are, for who we are.

I touched upon this in the previous conversation, but I want to go deeper here because complaining is a very seductive trap. Because there will always be someone who has something we don't have, and if we spend all our energy looking for what we don't have, we will surely find it. There will always be someone with more, seems happier, smarter, funnier, etc. and not just on social media but everywhere. Similar to exercise, dieting, or learning a new skill, we must practice habits that counter such negative reflexes. Step one is to complain way less! Change does not occur without repetition, practice and patience. The distance from my mind to my heart can sometimes feel miles long, yet I find that when I practice gratitude and patience, I recognize all I have to be grateful for. And when I focus on what I have already instead of what I lack, I feel how lucky I am. I find peace. I hang on to my connections and leave the tendency to whine in recovery (along with the wine.) I discover the tenderness of contentment. And the way to get there for me is not only to stop the complain–train but to practice gratitude instead as a way into my serenity.

A gratitude list I write down is a simple, perhaps overly used, but also useful tool I use daily. It's a routine I can rest in and lean on time after time to take stock of my blessings, from the small things like a hot cup of fresh coffee to the bigger things like my health. By focusing on recognition of all the positives in my life, I change how I feel about my life and how connected I feel to it. Often, I share this list with somebody else, but even just "saying it" to myself on the page helps tremendously. It is the first act of my day, a foundational part of my practice to live well, and it pushes me to be thankful even for my struggles and obstacles because they force me to grow. It encourages me to wonder what the purposes might be of my pain.

Though I can rarely make sense of why things happen or how God can explain why we have the struggles we do, I can use my voice to stay connected to God anyway. I do this by reminding myself and others we don't know the reasons for our hardships, and I also say that we *do* know the reason for our survival, which is to connect to life, to love, and to the joys of being here with other beings. A key way to stop complaining and start enjoying more is to stop asking the impossible "why" things happen and instead speak to one another and lean on one another as you go right through the situation to its other side. Be in the "what" without looking for the escape–clause of "why" –– there is none.

In today's world of convenience and endless scrolling, many of us lack inspiration, motivation and purpose in our efforts. Saying this out loud, just owning it, can break the spell of discontent and focus us instead on working at creating what we wish to feel within ourselves every day. That is how we tap into a sense of usefulness –– we go after it. As a famous golfer is said to have stated when asked for the secret of his success: "I was just lucky... the funny thing is that the harder I practice, the luckier I become." The more we actively seek, the more satisfied we will be, and hopefully, the more inspiration, motivation and purpose we will stumble upon. Because it's in the exerting, it's in the endeavoring that we build these states of mind in ourselves.

It requires us to surrender an attachment to immediate gratification. As Rabbi Jonathan Sacks says, we live in a world of silver bullets and instant change, a "what have you done for me lately" society. Any tool worth its value is not a silver bullet. It should demand from us our participation to merit it a worthy tool. Our involvement is what upgrades our outlook. We *do* it and keep doing it even when it takes a long time to show results. That's called perseverance, and it births resilience, both qualities I have discovered I learn exactly when I need to, which is when I have them at my disposal the least.

Question for You

So, back in Conversation Nine, we already got to work on writing a gratitude list. Now, let's commit to doing it for a week straight and see how that small act alone improves how we feel. If you're feeling brave, commit to a month! Over a month, I guarantee you'll feel amazing. I urge you to resist the urge to write the same things down if you're able. Think outside the box. This is nothing to phone in, this is how we leave our gripes behind and elevate into connectors. Think tiny and huge – a staple to hold papers together and the sun that warms your back. Challenge yourself to get creative and grow that list. Keep track of how many blessings are available to you in your life right now.

And then, here's the kicker with this next level of grateful living: share your list with somebody else. Maybe it's something you give and receive with a friend. Maybe you can start a text group thread of gratitude lists. Connect with others over the astonishing fullness that is contentment; I dare you.

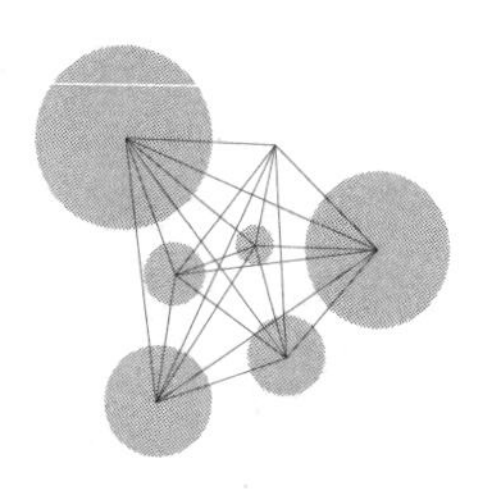

Conversation Twenty-Three: From Control to Flow

Who we live with and spend most of our time with has a huge impact on who we are. Once you connect with yourself, other people around you will feel it. And they will either get a jolt of energy because you're in the room as you are now, whole to yourself, or they will be upset by the changes. Maybe even threatened. That is okay—you are not here to control them. You are here to model what is possible. To be loving towards others by loving yourself, by letting yourself be loved, by embodying what it is like to connect, this is a brave act that leads by doing, and encourages others to connect too, when and if they're ready.

This entails staying "in flow," as I like to call it. Staying with that aligned feeling inside of you, speaking about it and holding it up high no matter who likes it or who does not. Connection happens as it's happening. Our loved ones will witness someone else emerge in us, but we will also see somebody else emerge in every person around us, as well as in the mirror because allowing flow and not succumbing to fear–based control changes our voice, our tone, and our views. The Higher Self in Us notices the Higher Self in Others. I'm not necessarily saying this will be a cinch, although it might be. Sometimes, it can be a struggle to feel ourselves while also being close to others. That is the information; it is the confirmation of the transformation. Where it's hard is where we are changing, where we are releasing our grip on predictability and comfort zones. We must choose connection over people pleasing or fear of evolving into our fullest expression.

Unfortunately, the ego will get louder as we decide not to spin about the future or dwell in the past or go through the mental checklist of who likes us; the ego doesn't give up. It won't stop speaking to us because it was born to keep us surviving, to protect us. Yet because you are dedicated to yourself, as the ego gets louder, connection will become your survival because different qualities, stronger qualities more affiliated with the real you, will morph you into a human of service and respect who seeks to control much less and flow with what life brings you much more. You will speak connection back to your ego, and it will drown out the sound of its alarm that tries to get your attention again, tries to repeat the tapes of old beliefs that kept you small and stuck, because by now, you love yourself. You love your life. And this sense of center will give you the faith it takes to choose connection over the sound of any alarm.

It's similar to *not* running out of a burning building because there is no fire. You are the building; you are not the one running out. You are intact, you are okay, you are safe, you have everything you ever needed inside because connection is your default setting. The fire is a ruse. We need not live as if we're controlling make–believe fires or putting out those started by somebody else. It's okay if it takes time for us to release our grip, our restraints and restrictions. We let go in little bits every single day until one day; we miss what we used to hang onto and the person we used to be when we were clutching onto the reigns for dear life. There is no need to rush to let go of control; there is no need to build a structure on top of a sloppy foundation. Flow is worth the time to merge with. Any time we lose our footing, we learn how to stay standing and balanced, how to focus on the solid beam, dancing with what life gives us because flow feels good. It is the most remarkable byproduct of saying things rooted in connection, and in realizing it is safe to wildly release into flow.

Just look out your window. Things are growing and blooming, things are dying and enriching, life is happening, and it has its rhythm, its intelligence. We don't decide what and when. There is an abundance of that same frequency in you, in every breath. It is simply our job to move with the river. Anything that keeps us not in flow is not meant for us in connection. The way to overcome the insidious need to control is to spend even a few minutes every day with our family and friends, our inner circle, as authentically as we can. Genuine. Feeling. Together. Nothing in the way, nothing between you, nothing separating you. No lectures. No manipulations. No agenda. No motivations. Being, sharing the inside of each moment together as it unfolds, seeing what happens as the seconds tick. Unpredictable. Surprising. This is how to practice flow.

Being present is an act for those you love, and it is also an act of love for yourself. It is an act of connecting to everything. The presence you share with those you care about is the highest form of love you can offer them as well as yourself. Being in the room with the ones you love, really IN THE ROOM, will allow you speak honestly and purely about what is really on your mind or in your heart. This lets us know others and to be known by others. This is how we can be loved in return. Changing our beliefs cannot happen without increasing our presence, and presence changes our beliefs. So, as we practice flowing one tiny next step at a time, we start to give of ourselves differently, and pretty soon, there will be nothing else we have to do but this because it alone will melt away the dark corners of our minds. When connected, we attract everything meant for us because we are our most vibrant. Our energy becomes clean and easy to magnetize. Everything will work for us in this way of living because there is no other reality. Nothing is against us. We realize nothing ever was.

Isn't life grand? When we're swimming in its grandness, moving towards what is designed for us as everything else drifts away. When we're looking up at the sun, the moon, the stars, the clouds. And what happens when we hit rocks? We go with it, we learn from it, we turn over the tipped boat and get back in. Because the birds are swirling and calling, and it's our right to laugh with them, to float, to find peace in floating as an act of connection itself, and let go of the desire to bend water to our will by persuading and coercing. There is nothing we need to do in this state of mind but enjoy the ride.

Question for You

I want to ask you now: What can you let go of? Where can you stop controlling? Pull out a piece of paper and just start there, imagining a dandelion flower as that thing, person, idea, or goal and blow it to the wind. Blow it away. Let it be, set it free. Set yourself free. What flow can come into your life if you did so? Because hindsight is always twenty–twenty. If we are lucky enough to live into old age, we will inevitably ask what is important, and most people I've talked to share that it's family and friendship, it's connection. So instead of waiting to wonder why you didn't live your life differently, why you didn't spend more time with others being instead of maneuvering, not worrying but loving, you can actually do it now. You can talk to yourself from your "Future You," an imagined seat that allows you still to ask yourself: How do I want to live before I die? Before I grow old? How can I get away from any identity that keeps me from that when it matters so much less?

Listen to your older, wiser self and heed your words. Let go of the controlling ego and flow with what counts most in your life today. Write that letter from your older, wiser self, and if you're perhaps if you're feeling it, write back to this future you with all the love and appreciation in your heart. You are connected to this You already.

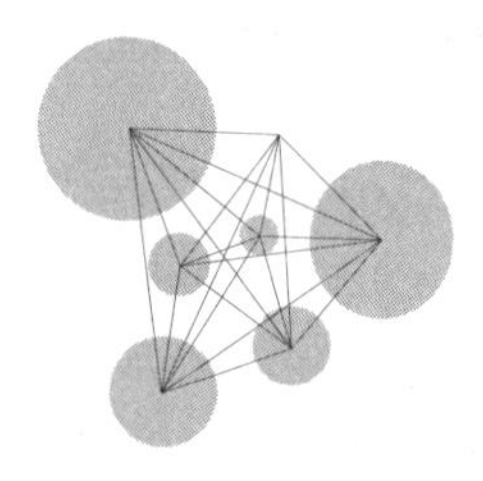

Conversation Twenty–Four: From Filtered to Authentic

After spending almost a week with a group of high–level healers, I learned two personal lessons that will have a life-long impact on me if I stay accountable to them.

The first lesson was that essence precedes form. My interpretation of that was when I have awareness of myself being disingenuous, to say out loud: "I'm not living authentically." Sometimes, this feels less overwhelming—to speak it – than to figure out how to live authentically because I don't always know how to define that. If I commit to calling myself out and reminding myself daily, I will honor it by claiming it, I will be accountable, the form will come, and the details will crystalize. By paying attention and stating my authenticity as a priority, the form will follow, and I'll be able to act on it without forcing it. Forcing isn't a move towards connection anyway.

The second lesson I learned was only to use words that make me feel good. To speak kindly to myself, and avoid using words that cause me shame. Because from a shamed place, I also can't connect, not with myself and not with you. So, to apply the second lesson to the first lesson, the word "authentic" may not be the right word for me. I can change that to "living above the line or below the line," or I can use "sincere" instead. The key is to find the words that motivate me from a positive perspective, that demonstrate to myself that I care about how I feel. To add to this, when speaking with our loved ones or anyone, we can also dedicate ourselves to trying to find the words that *they* prefer and understand, that they appreciate. This is how we motivate others – coming from a place of connection and acknowledgment while making them feel cared for and seen. Because so often it's not what we say but what is heard that makes the difference in our relationships.

Being intentional with our words changes the nature of how we speak to ourselves and to others. It may be the pause we need to connect with our Higher Selves, or it may be what an intention is designed for, which is to slow us down and connect inside before we try to connect outside with our words. To merge with our words, we say what we mean and mean what we say.

During the Jewish holiday of Passover, which is a holiday that commemorates God bringing the Jewish people out of slavery and into freedom, I like to express my gratitude for all of my freedoms, even if I am still a slave to my mind.

This is a more emotional type of slavery, yet one I must consciously work on to remain free. I am transparent and genuine in my celebration of freedom. I share with those close how I am still enslaved in my head, how I still filter myself, especially around materialism, something I struggle with constantly. It's easy for me to believe (and sometimes to say) that I would be much happier if I had more stuff. In speaking it out loud, though, I free myself even a little bit because that is not authentically who my soul is.

My bondage is usually two–fold: it is my attachment to materialism, and it also measures my insides against other's outsides. This robs me of using my tools to overcome my hang–ups and keeps me in a loop where I filter myself, edit myself, hide myself, and bury myself in a feeling that ultimately leads to unworthiness. If I don't break the cycle, if I don't speak truth to my experience, especially during a time of deep reflection about how our people were not free, then it gets harder and harder for me to identify my sincere truth and live by it. Attachments hinder authenticity sometimes because I interpret them as chains. I think that to stay close to a person or a thing. I have to be the man that person or thing <u>needs</u> from me. This is an antonym for being somebody who trusts themselves and can respond to their inner call to be the individual they are. However, they change and grow and become.

Only attachments that see us as our best, that push us towards being our purest selves, and that encourage our evolution can foster connection. If not, those same attachments become authenticity killers. They tie us down and back. They cause us to barter and beg so we can keep what we must hold onto to be okay, when what we must hold on to be okay is our voice. That voice always pleads for freedom.

Stop trying to filter what you say, how you say it, what you don't say, and what you will tolerate others saying around you to be accepted or approved of, to get a like or a high–five. Be you. Be a whistleblower. Be the one who says NO. Be the one who says YES. Speak mostly with—and listen mostly to – the whisper that knows who you are, the Real You that was simultaneously there when you were a kid and that has never been arrived at because you are still becoming that you now. Authenticity is the same you and the changing you.

This is the genuine connection that every other relationship relies on because no connections outside of us will ever make up for the one we don't have inside.

Question for You

Prayer has been my greatest armor against my own self–imposed "slavery." By that, I mean prayer in whatever form feels right for you – again, making this exercise a touchstone for authenticity. How do you like to pray? While talking to God in the shower? Dancing? Singing? Surfing? Free writing in your journal? Going to a service? Telling your dog? Hiking on a mountain? That is the exercise I bring to you now, an opportunity to feel out natural, comfortable ways for you to pray.

To define the word prayer by focusing on the first lesson I mentioned above—by focusing essence to discover form. Or, by implementing the second lesson and using a different word, a kind one for you, and whatever it is, practicing it here. Maybe prayer is contemplation for you, or singing, or Reiki energy. You decide. No need to filter. This is an exercise for deeper connection because to connect with those we are meant to connect with, we must be who we are, who we are proud to be, by respecting ourselves first and most in all of our iterations.

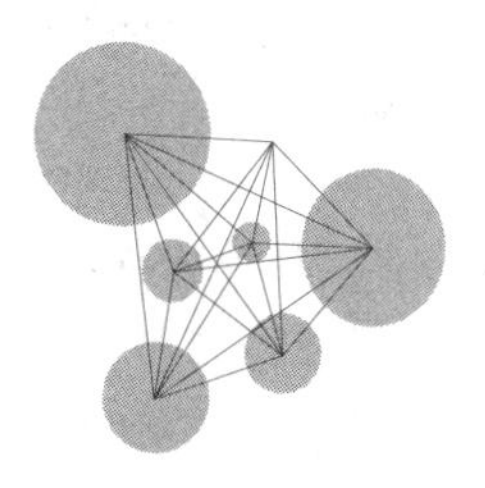

Conversation Twenty Five: From Blame to Boundaries

We blame capitalism and fake news. We blame the Internet, social media, our mothers and fathers. We blame the ex, the Universe not being on our side; we blame the dog who ate our homework. The more we blame, the more we disconnect. The more we identify as a hater, the more we disconnect. The blame game is a rigged game. No matter what position you play, for which team, or when or how, you lose.

We are living in a world that feeds on blame and disconnection because that's how they get us to buy more stuff and search outside ourselves for answers and fight one another instead of enjoying the natural world and the Spirit all around us, instead of combining forces. We must create boundaries around our connection to nourish it, nurture it, and keep it safe. Nobody else and nothing else can be more important. Blame is what you go to when you have no boundaries. It is a cheap replacement for boundaries. Blame spoken out loud is a contagious poison of shared limiting beliefs that disempower everyone around it. Collectively, blame causes us to wait for somebody or something outside of us change or do right by us... yet what if they never do? Boundary setting is nothing short of honorable and courageous. It is a way to reconnect to life and to the life you want to live without waiting on anybody, without giving our power away. Why would we when there is a Higher Power with us, in us?

The root of the word boundary in Hebrew is almost the same as the root of the word heroism. The brave and the heroic cannot be tamed, told to shut up and follow mindlessly. Those with boundaries can't either, for they listen to their internal wishes and, at some point, refuse to tread water so they can focus on where they want to go. And they protect that vision, they feed it. They are too busy tending to themselves to waste time pointing fingers when it does little for them or their forward momentum.

Set blame aside. Who started what when where can sit in a drawer. Your work to do, if you decide to do it, is inside, it is being true to the picture of how you want your reality to go, and then it is protecting that like a hero does so you can walk out the door and into the manifestation of how you want to feel. Draw boundaries around that feeling and claim it as your right. Connect to your dream, your imagination, and let go of the speeches about who or what to blame for what you are continuing to be limited by.

Being aware of what keeps you feeling alive and full of energy, you can draw lines in the sand that keep you that way and that keeps away anybody or anything that dulls your aliveness. This is scary. It means possibly losing people and things. It means if things don't work out, you will have nobody to blame but *yourself*. Still do it. Because that's the thing: you think you will blame yourself if you fail; you will not. Because in taking accountability, you develop all the skills you need to be proud of yourself for trying. You become strong enough to fight through that human tendency, that misbelief, that trap because you can never actually blame yourself for listening to your truth. You can be disappointed when you don't get what you want, and it's somebody else's fault, but that's because you're actually angry that you gave away your life. To know you have kept yourself well by answering to yourself, that's the way it goes when we use boundaries around ourselves, our mission, and how we want to look at the world.

When we have boundaries, we don't blame anybody because by blaming others, we unintentionally decide that we are helpless. By blaming others, we only confirm that we have no choices, that our voices are squashed and our needs too. Then we never move forward at all—why would we? It is difficult to look at this, trust me, I know. We live in a society that regards mistakes and failures as abominations when they couldn't be further from that. Mistakes and failures are huge billboards of bravery—they mean you did something, you tried something, you heard yourself, you dreamed!

We have the courage to life in accordance with our inner guidance system, we have the courage to draw boundaries with anybody who aims to get us to abandon our inner guidance system by distracting us with rage. We realize that boundaries are nothing more than tentpoles from God, they are spiritual check–ins, ways to stay with ourselves when life or people try to pull us apart We won't hemorrhage our energy anymore when we recognize that blame is a sophisticated way to spin our gears and go nowhere.

Be willing to let them blame you. To blame you for having boundaries that make you fight for connection. Because if other people in your life are not your heroes or your wrongdoers, if you're not in the chorus of shouting, others who are might blame you. This is their attempt to bring you down, force you to cross your lines, to get back in line and go back to who you were without boundaries because that version of you served them better. Can you feel how valiant you must be here to resist this? Siding with our boundaries by knowing what they are and honoring them is knight–worthy. It makes for connectable humans. Others like us—others with courage—will be drawn to us. It is worth the shift.

You might think being born into an Orthodox Jewish family with a father who was a leading rabbi in the Jewish community might have given me a shortcut to a relationship with a Power who is greater than me. The opposite was true. I felt disconnection from day one in my highly religious family ironically, and so addiction was inevitable. I did not receive the warmth of my faith even though it comforted and inspired my parents and siblings. God was based in fear and shame and conditional love, which paved the way for me to feel really badly about myself. To feel disconnected. By the time I was 33-years-old, those bad feelings had led me so far away from faith, I didn't even know who I was other than a drunk and an addict, surrounded by the emptiness that comes when you don't believe in anything or anyone, especially not yourself. When you're sure nobody in the world loves you, nobody in the world could love you, when you think to yourself, *If they knew me, they would hate me.*

I hated myself. And I blamed everybody in the world, especially those closest, especially God, for the way I hated me. I did not have a faith personal to me with boundaries around it that kept it safe, cherished, and mine. I was following what others told me to believe and then blaming them when I didn't like my life or my internal state. That is the epitome of disconnection. My faith was in pieces, and the pieces were not only gone, they were nowhere to be found. And it was the best thing that has ever happened because it made me have to be brave. Brave or die.

What came next is a familiar story: rock bottom, working a 12–Step program, treatment, sobriety. Eventually, after my healing, I got into the recovery business so I could offer the same chance for transcendent rehabilitation to others. I began to connect once again to the faith that had scared me and scarred me. I went full circle once I understood that I can redefine what God meant, even design an idea of God that worked for me. And it worked, I built myself my shelter that kept me safe. I created boundaries around it.

Years later, I found myself at my son's Bar Mitzvah, so many decades after my own, and I turned to my father and said: "I didn't want to be religious because of you. I didn't *not* want to be religious, in case you were right. Little did I know that you'd end up being my greatest teacher. You gave unconditional love to Jewish youth, and I now give unconditional love to people who recover from addiction."

And I was happy. I stopped blaming him. I had boundaries. I can invite him in.

By allowing myself to make God personal, I allowed myself to live close to that God, and to draw boundaries around my relationships and boundaries around myself. Allowing myself to discover the ways I was more like my father than not like him did not mean I forgave him for every offense or pretended the pain between us didn't happen. It meant I was choosing to connect with him and build pathways of connection *for myself.* I did it for me, not for him, because it was part of my healing. I searched to believe differently than him so I can realize we were similar. I do the same line of work my father did, just for different people. He dedicated his passion to help Jewish youth, and I give it to those who suffer from nebulous, amorphous monsters, we addicts. We dear, dear addicts. Aren't we all addicts by now? Isn't the opposite of connection addiction? Can we ever have faith if we don't earn it, if we're not courageous enough to make it our own so we can appreciate it?

Years later, I was sharing the story of that conversation with my father in front of 500 people, and an important distinction hit me. It hit me as a helper, and I share it with all helpers who are willing to hear it: what I should have said to my father is, "you *received* love from Jewish youth, and I *receive* it from addicts." Because as helpers, the truth is we give but we also receive so much love. The point of the love is to affect how we show up with those who matter the most. It's not about the people we serve. It's about the people we serve helping us in return for helping them, so we understand the importance of showing up for our families. Because of these connections inside myself, I can show up as the father I want to be, the one my kids deserve.

Question for You

As a person who runs a recovery center, I have had the great privilege of witnessing close up how people get well. Across the treatment centers I have founded, through both inpatient and outpatient programs, I know what it takes for someone who comes into our centers nearly dead to emerge with life again, with vitality and love bursting from within them. It is the ability to know oneself, to be loyal to that knowing, and to trust oneself while also being the guard of the boundaries that keep that sacred knowing intact. Every addict I know who is in recovery is my hero. To go on living, they blame nobody, take full responsibility, and take their own lives back.

Now, tell me about you...who do you blame? How can you take your life back, draw boundaries around what you decide is meant for you, and connect with all that is waiting for you on the other side?

Sometimes, we believe boundaries are cruel. That they keep people out or make us selfish, but nothing can be further from reality. Boundaries model for others how to clean our internal house, how to keep that house clean, and how to rest in it, grateful for the house at all. We take care of the things we appreciate and love, don't we? Boundaries say *I take care of me.*

Boundaries mean it's not anybody else's job or fault, when I don't.

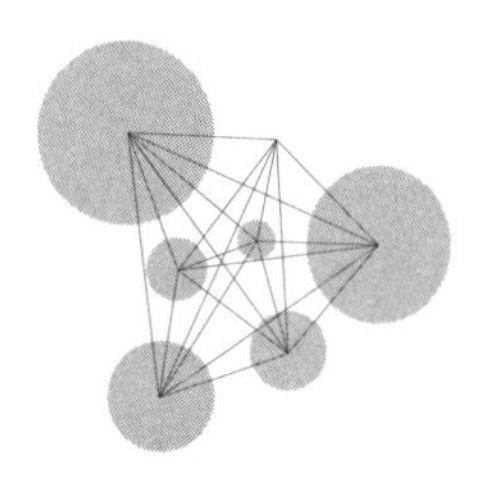

Conversation Twenty–Six: From Desperation to Intuition

It is undeniably important that we seek to practice empathy and kindness for others and their struggles. Yet, nobody talks about at what point the empathy becomes toxic, and the kindness becomes inappropriate. Where is the line between making people around us happy to attain connection and people–pleasing at the expense of what makes us happy?

We live in a world of polarization, and I am here to tell you it is difficult to engage in productive conversations when we buy into black–or–white thinking. It makes us desperate. It makes us believe, even if unconsciously, that we are justified in our selfishness so we don't become doormats or that we shall lay down our lives mired in codependency to accrue love points from the people around us by constantly seeking their validation. It makes us think we should turn the other cheek when we're punched or smacked back. It's not either or. It's not binary. Much exists between those ends of the extremes, and it can change constantly. That's why we need to plug into our intuition.

Because it's a daily process, and it requires responsiveness to check in, assess, reassess, and adjust intuitively each day what we need and what we can give. This lets us deplane from the desperation flight we're on all the time, whether we're desperate to make ourselves happy and finally fill up or desperate to please others and win their favor. Desperation keeps us clawing and chasing, focused outside of ourselves, and highly disconnected. Desperation is rooted in lack. When connected to a Higher Self, we can hear desperation falter. We can hear a real voice that knows what we need. Intuition can be another name for connection to that voice or to Something More. This lets us maintain empathy for others who might be suffering without letting that compassion become a hindrance for ourselves.

Because if we don't count to ourselves, how can we possibly feel connected and fulfilled? Who then is taking care of you if you are obsessed and consumed with taking care of everybody else? How do we determine if our empathy and kindness is descending into the realm of enabling, a byproduct of desperation that actually disempowers others, which is not our goal when we care so much? Balance is a real thing. It is an intuitive thing.

While nothing, almost nothing, in the current climate encourages us to go inward, I hope if there's one thing you take away from this book, it's that time with your being, time listening to what your gut feeling is saying to you, is essential for living a gratifying life. *Both* are possible here – the nonbinary. Balance is possible here, too. Yes, it is so very important that we help others and hold space for what they are going through, yet when it is harmful to ourselves, and when we are not keeping our personal well full, we cannot effectively be of service to anyone anymore. We cannot give from empty. When we do, we give toxic fumes.

I am also of the belief that if we are not open to a dialogue intended to inspect, investigate, and flush out if our actions are helpful or harmful, if we find ourselves being wounded and defensive instead, then this is the first clue we have gone astray from our good intentions. Because the intuitive seat lives open for introspection and investigation, it lives as a malleable conductor for whatever is pulsing with connection <u>now</u>. If we are taking the correct actions, then our motives don't actually even factor in, do they? Our truth merges there, but not our agendas.

Look, I have struggled with people–pleasing for my entire life, always living in fear that if I said no to something or chose to disagree with you, you will no longer like me. I lived under the misguided narrative that if I rocked the boat, you will either immediately or ultimately determine me unworthy of your love and then kick me out of the boat. However, I was living unaware that when I said yes to something that my gut screamed NO, what I was doing was showing myself that I was unlovable! So yeah, it was a fear I had fulfilled the prophecy of by doing it subconsciously to myself, already keeping love away from myself as I implored you to give it to me instead. It is not your job. It was never your job. Intuition is an inside job based in self–love.

Empathy reaches poisonous levels when it begins to affect personal health or when held back from learning our lessons because of fixers and enablers. When we try to fix things for the people we care about, all we're doing eventually is hurting them, preventing them from building resilience and perspective as we hold them back from experiencing their journey. That's for us, not for them. That's their path, not ours. That's a sneaky attempt to boost and serve our egos. This doesn't mean we shouldn't care – remember, both/and is intuition and either/or is desperation. One helps with true connection, and the other festers on making you feel as bad as it can.

Empathy, kindness, and people–pleasing are all on display for me personally when I am giving advice to others because who am I to know what is best for somebody else? My job is not to tell someone the correct actions to take but to help them listen to their intuition, to guide them in ridding themselves of the desperate spiral of personal self–doubt. When I am doing my best work, I serve less as an arbiter of truth and more as a supporter and a conduit. A cheerleader and a safety net. But never as The Answer.

Question for You

Your turn. What are signs you are people–pleasing or seeped in desperate behaviors that keep you lost from your inner knowing? As you move forward, what behaviors can you remember that might be barometers for you to stop, reconnect with yourself, and unchain yourself from your ego so you can be engaged enough to join the world?

The journey you undergo with your intuition is a great way to face your fears of self–judgment and to imagine what your life might be like if you believed the people around you loved you with no sort of expectation or because you do anything for them. That literally *is* how you love yourself.

You just love yourself. You hear yourself. You are here for yourself.

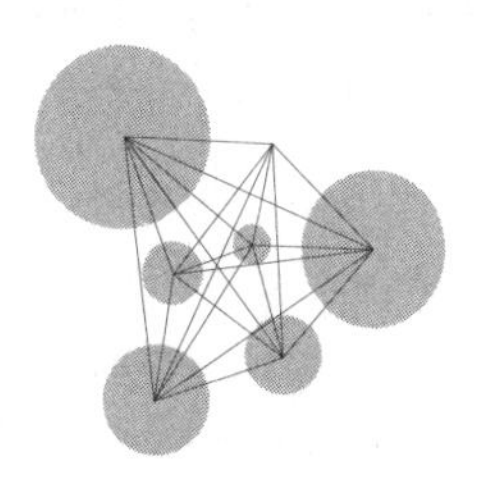

Conversation Twenty-Seven: From Defensive to Acceptance

Every week, I read inspiring words from different scholars, leaders, healers and religious thinkers. They talk about freedom, about what it takes to get there, and about the culture where everybody's opinion is valid, legit, and matters.

All around us today, there is extreme hatred and destruction, riots, looting, and violence. These methods of defensiveness and chaos do not work to bring forth change. Education remains the key to solving our biggest problems. Though it takes time and patience, though often arduous, it's in educating our children that we need to always listen to one another, that's how we will find our way towards true freedom. People must feel safe enough to express their opinions without judgment so we can guide them and learn new perspectives through their narratives or shed light on our outlook and pain. It is back and forth, never one way but two. This requires a colossal amount of acceptance.

Acceptance of the time it takes and of the process itself. Acceptance that others will disagree with you. Acceptance about discourse and even dislike, but still staying within civility as everybody has the right to express themselves so that, ultimately, we can find our way towards connection. Real connection excludes no one. Through our words, our chants, our shouts and our catchy slogans, if we only aimed at connection instead of division, if we only made room for everybody instead of defending our position as the correct one, wouldn't we be in a better place as a society?

I am reminded of a story about the great leader Nelson Mandela. When he was in jail, the guards were instructed to brutally beat him daily. However, every time they came to his cell, Mr. Mandela would still greet these guards with a smile, telling them he knew that they were only doing as they were instructed. After a few weeks of his unflinching kindness and his enormous tolerance in the face of their brutality, the guards refused to beat him anymore. While I am not expecting any of us to turn the other cheek in this way or take whipping and beating, it is extreme proof that through acceptance, through education, a smile, kindness, tolerance, through being the source of connection we wish the world would give to us, we can affect lasting change. Hate, harm, and violence create a cycle of more hate, harm, and violence and nothing more. This is disconnection at its pinnacle, and it never works to grow the world or leave harmony in its wake.

We say in the 12–Step rooms that expectations are resentments waiting to happen. I can attest to this. Though we all have expectations, sometimes, the simple act of voicing them robs them of their power to cause resentment and destroy our relationships. Defensiveness tells us we shouldn't have to ask; somebody should read our mind. Acceptance nudges us to ask for what we need, knowing we might get it, but at the very least, we will be done with the expectation with the power to trouble us. It's not for us to expect anything of anybody. It's for us to ask, fill our buckets, and support others in filling theirs. To take it a step further, usually an indirect benefit of popping expectations' bubbles is that you also release the charge of extreme emotions, which aren't healthy for finding commonality and compromise. It's extremes that can be deadly. If we want connection and want to live in peace, it's all about creating a happy medium, a space where everyone is heard.

The question then becomes, how do we accomplish this? How do we make a bigger landing pad in the middle? Especially in a world threatening to pull us all apart from one another religiously, politically, and materially. It's up to us, each of us, me writing and you reading this book to reestablish and hold the center that has been lost.

Maimonides, like Aristotle, believed that emotional intelligence comes from balancing excess and deficiency, not too much and not too little. Too much fear makes me a coward; too little makes me rash and foolhardy, the guy who takes unnecessary risks. (I've been both.) But the middle way is courageous because it allows for other colors to get into black and white thinking. That is how portraits are made.

Maimonides made two exceptions in his work: pride and anger. He said that even a little pride (some Sages suggested as little as "an eighth of an eighth") is too much. He stated the same about anger, which is the final conclusion of most resentments. When anger causes us to harden or lose control, or when it's based on self–interest, it is nothing short of awful. It offers no value when anger becomes an impenetrable wall, the same wall that shares a room with pride. There is no way to connect to somebody in that headspace. Resistance, rejection, self–righteousness and refusal are all antonyms for acceptance. It is acceptance of what is and what can be forged together that will let us form a union.

All people on this planet – all beings with life and hearts and souls – we are all one organism. We are all needed, and we are all important, and just because we don't always see eye to eye doesn't mean we can't find a way to love each other, be friends, or at the very least coexist within the bond of assembly. Me coming to you, you coming, and a string of pearls gets strung one jewel at a time. The more people who take hands, the longer we will reach, the stronger we will be fastened to one another, and the truer we will make this world as it was intended to be: a place for all of creation to experience what life has to offer. Shields and swords down, no need for offense or defense. As we say in the Big Book of Alcoholics Anonymous, "Acceptance is the answer to every problem today."

Question for You

My question for you is this: ask yourself, can you let people be entitled to their opinions, even if you don't like them, and can you listen? Can you be careful to acknowledge each person's humanity and then share your opinions with them in the most respectful, loving manner possible as a form of education that has the power to shift, repair, and save the world? Can you allow that back from them?

We are all seeking the same thing—safety and security. So many of us are going about it in ways that will destroy both safety and security, both for ourselves and each other. Isn't there a better way? If we are connected, won't you support me, and I will support you? This is where we can most easily connect, can't we see that? When everybody moves towards the same spot, nobody has to give all the way.

This isn't an idea of nirvana or only for hippies. It is possible for all of us.

PART FOUR

WHAT WE EMBODY

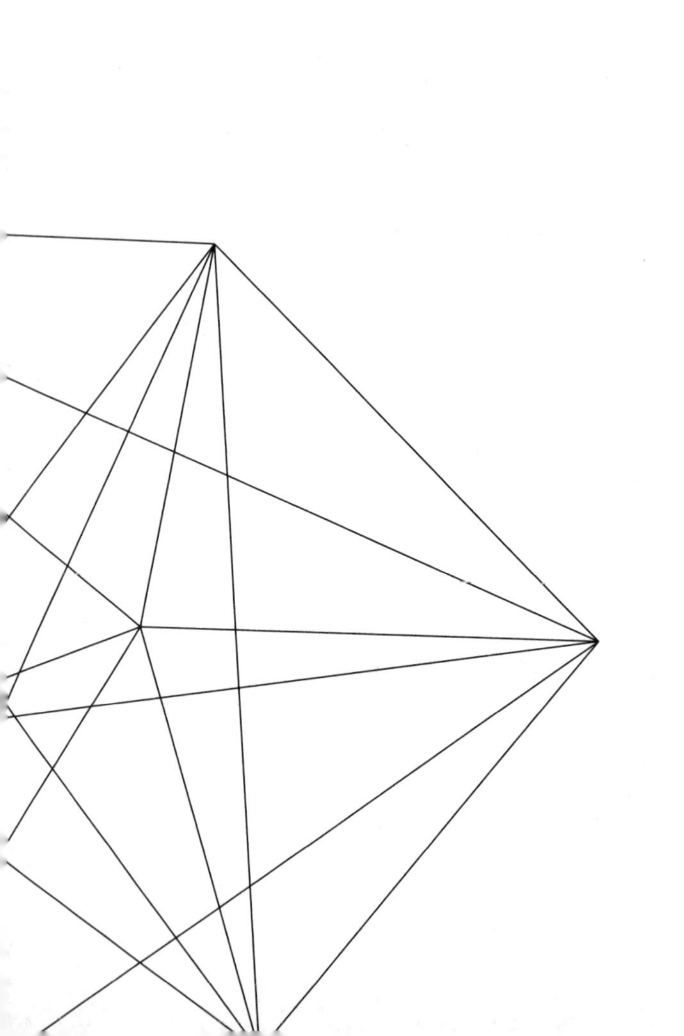

We've dug into what we believe, what we do, and what we say. When we put it all together, we are left with what we embody. Embodiment is what we stand for, what we exemplify; it is our essence. It is a three–hundred–sixty–degree measurement, holistic and cohesive; it is this earthly plane and beyond it, above it, and below it.

God gave us commandments. God understands human nature. God knows that we need to be guided to the truth and given leeway to keep striving so we can continue to step into ourselves. It happens on its own time. A famous quote comes to mind: "Death is hard for the living." Death is hard for the living because the dead are resting in peace, but the rest of us still here are daring to turn away from the Times Square of our heads to be made multi–dimensional. We still have so much work to do from within our human suits, while those who have passed, their souls are moving on, so it's only a physical loss they've experienced. Thus, it's felt only by those left behind in the physical – us.

Life is so much more than what we see. I'm not only talking about faith and love and gravity, I'm also talking about embodiment. About the stuff in us that twists and turns and grows and blooms. The stuff that keeps us fighting and weeping and connecting with ourselves, each other and a power greater than us. To be embodied is to go invisible. We go in. We go on. We line up from tip to toe.

I like to think of being embodied as baking. Stay with me. It's almost as if I am constantly dough. New ingredients being mixed, often the same ingredients even if they feel different today, but malleable and delicious. When I'm not embodied, it's not that I am cooked, I'm trying to keep it together and not lose my flour everywhere. When I am not put together well or for real, I cannot do all the things we've discussed, believing, behaving and speaking from a connected place, from a true place, imperfectly but striving and trusting that I can, that I'm not alone. Being mindful about embodiment and even trying is all I have to do. When I am dough sliding into the heat—not half-baked or cooked but ready—I can feel it.

That's what this part of the book is about: feeling ready. Ready to stand for something and personify our realness, inside and out. How to get there? How to emit the energy of what you are? By being it. All the parts combined, it's where things overlap. It's in the combining itself. It's in the space between parts. This is what we're referring to – embodiment is all of it, and the gray matter that fills in what is not all of it as well.

It has been proven that being thankful prolongs life by as much as seven years. In 2001, a study looked at the lives of about 700 nuns. Astoundingly, it was found those who were focused on what they had, what they were blessed with and thankful for, those who embodied the love and gratitude they preached, this led them like a sharp laser light to living longer than those who didn't. We have to strive to transform into the product of all this work, to let it be our lifeblood, let it come first and most. Embodiment is not half-assed. It is not wishy-washy. It is the crux of the matter, the culmination of everything made manifest for a seed to blossom and thrive.

You become your plant, your flower. None other like you.

And so you've entered your territory now. This unchartered terrain is just yours, and the map is being drawn as you move through it. I'm not saying this to intimidate you, I'm saying it to emphasize how incredible you are. You are both the explorer and the guide, the one with answers and the one with questions. You are in front and behind, and you are sometimes walking, sometimes running, sometimes sitting to take in the view. Still, you are finding your way into a courageous new world within yourself as you put it all together, mixing the tonic that results in your frequency, and then drinking it, adjusting the chemicals for next time. You know you best. You present that to the world.

The vibration of who you are that we feel when we meet you, that's what we're digging into now. It precedes you in the room, and it will linger long after you go.

This is the most connected time of your life. Congratulations! Though it may not be all daisy and daffodils every step of the way, the path is breathtaking, the weather is stunning, and you will learn to get back up again when you trip or scrape a knee.

You've arrived to arriving. You've earned your place here. You are the you'est you that you could ever be.

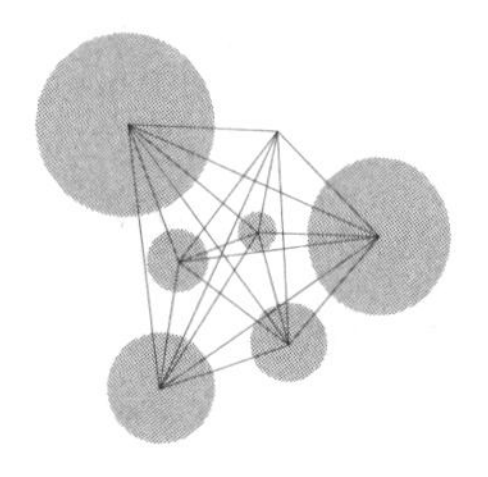

Conversation Twenty-Eight: From Reactive to Intentional

When seeking connection, when we are open to connection, and our antennas are up for it, we don't simply react to the world and other people; rather, we pause. Because reactions come without thought, without spirit, without intention. Intention is the only thing we can control, and it lets us stay with the desired outcome of connecting. That's right, intention syncs us up to what we come to a situation or conversation for, it focuses us on what we bring, what we hope to add or learn. Intention is an overall idea we can use like a flashlight to guide us in life. Now, how things will actually go? That's way beyond us; that's never in our control. We can uphold an intention that keeps us grounded in connecting.

When we live our lives with intent, no matter how things

go, we can, at the very least rest knowing that we have maintained our objective, that we kept offering ourselves up for connection by being true to a purpose. This is nothing short of holy, a way of acting worthy of respect because it doesn't demand it.

Sage Hillel said, "If I'm not for myself, who is for me? And if I'm only for myself, then who am I?" When I cannot think of an intention for myself, when I am confused about my aim or how to show up in the world, I think of those words. I think of how they provide a tightrope for connection, just enough tension to keep me connected to myself and others, and then I try to walk that rope as I meet up with somebody or even walk out my door.

When I'm my most reactive, though, I respond in a way that is more than likely anti–connection and will often cause me regret later on. It's those hotheaded responses rooted in my fears, insecurities, and unaccounted emotions that block me from being my best self, the kind of man people want to know. Reactive is how I behave when I am the least aware, least mindful, and least bonded to my Higher Power and myself. The Bible suggests each of us can be holy. As the verse states, "Let us make humans in our image," it doesn't single out one specific person, but every human as created in a Godly image. So we are all holy inside. We all have it in us to pulse with an intention that touches on that holiness, day in and day out. So the question becomes: What can we do to remain in that state of holiness, which is our natural, default setting? The answer boils down to humility, which is a factor in all my greatest intentions.

True humility is believing that I'm not greater than or less than anybody else. I am holy, just as you are holy. You are worthy, like I am worthy. I'm as responsible for my actions as you are responsible for yours; neither of us is any better or any worse. From this frame of mind, my intentions can lead my behavior instead of my reactions because equality is already established. We all know the saying, "The road to hell was paved with good intentions." It's been taken out of context. Having good intentions that guide us can keep us humble. Having humility to guide us can keep us married to holy intentions. If we stay true to them, if they actually mean something to us, there is no reason to believe we'd be led to hell.

However, *saying* we have good intentions but not living up to them does not and cannot serve us because the intentions are not beacons we follow. They aren't committed acts, rather, we still plan to react however we want to. If false intentions don't actually influence our behavior, if they don't factor in humility, then it doesn't matter what they are or what we "intend" because it's not curbing or crafting what we do. Our intentions should come before our reactions. They should shape us. That is how we embody connection. That is how we embody holiness.

A person is known in three circumstances: When intoxicated, when they are angry, and lastly, when they deal with money. Under each circumstance, our inhibitions are lifted, and true colors are shown. I think in all these areas, we need to first steer our intentions towards the work we need to do, pay attention to where we are struggling, and see ourselves without judgment or labeling. If we remain lovable no matter what, especially during these heated and intense scenarios—drinking, fury, and finances—then we can remember that everybody else remains lovable, too. We can breathe into our own regulating hands and call to mind an intention that connects us to the living experiment. Then, we can leave immature, dysregulated, chaotic, messy, sloppy reactions behind and be there for ourselves and others. I can't think of anything more humble or holy than that.

If ego drove my behavior, I'd be screwed. Because my ego usually works in two ways: It either tells me I'm better than somebody and I can get away with something, or more often, it tells me I'm worse and what's the point in trying, they're better, and I'm a loser. Or it tells me to prove myself and to hurry up about it because I've been less than for so long. None of these scenarios are a connecting way to live, are they? The intention I hold onto to live by the words of Hillel above reminds me that I'm responsible for me, I'm right–sized, and so is everyone else. Equality shuts the ego right up in my experience. Equal allows us all to accept our gifts, our challenges, our successes and our failures, and then to behave in a responsible, humble manner that accepts other people's gifts, challenges, successes and failures. Simply put, this is showing up, no matter what, as others do.

We are all lovable because we are. We don't need to buy into the negative thoughts or self–talk the mind tries to sell us, nor shall we buy anything outside of us either. A toy made to offer fake promises can magically make everything better. You do that for you now.

Question for You

We all wear masks to protect ourselves and to fool ourselves or others so we can make life something other than what I've laid out. We want to be more to feel like enough. This is a surefire way to lose hold of our emotions and fly off the handle. That's why the exercise in this chapter is a tool of regulation. Self–regulating means we track our bodies, we notice our feelings, and we tend to take care of ourselves first so we don't overreact or respond from a triggered place. Try it with me now, won't you?

Take stock of how you're feeling in this moment, to notice what is here for you right now. Then, put one hand on your chest if you can, and put your other hand somewhere on your stomach. Take long, slow, deep breaths trying to move both hands, trying to breathe equally into not only your front but also your back. Make both those hands rise. After a few rounds, take inventory again. Now, how do you feel and what is present for you? What sensations are alive in your body? This small act is a way to regulate, and when combined with an intention, it can keep you and your behavior on track. It can keep you connected to yourself, your body and your needs, and because you are full and loving yourself, then you will be more than capable of connecting to others as well. From here, you don't need somebody else to act any which way, you don't need anything to go a certain way, you don't need to be filled up by anyone or anything. You might like it, but you are okay regardless. Embodying in your body that you are okay to yourself, is living aligned with intention and humility. I especially use this tool to remove a mask when I realize I am wearing one and pretending.

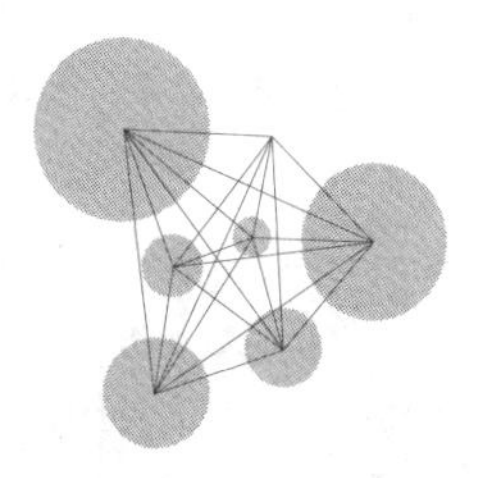

Conversation Twenty–Nine: From Judgement to Observer

Depression, addiction, compulsions, anxiety... I have often heard from those who either don't struggle with their mental health or don't admit to themselves that they struggle with their mental health, something to the tune of: "Why can't these people summon the willpower just to stop and be happy? They're so selfish. Get over it!"

As someone who has struggled with the issues above, let me start by saying we wish we could get over it. We wish our minds didn't fill us with negative stories. We wish we weren't panicking. We wish we didn't need to find short–term self–medicators for long–term issues. Shame is actually the greatest factor in continuing our negative behaviors. Shame is our greatest barrier to getting help, and it is rooted in judgment – yours and our own.

It does not benefit anyone to tell them to get over how they feel. It implies that we are inconvenienced, and it implies that we are exasperated when we could be compassionate and connected to them instead. Simply holding space for another by giving them a chance to share inside our presence is all the empathy often required. It is what constitutes a significant helping hand. Now I didn't say let others do whatever they want and let them get away with it. What I mean is, what does it cost us to let somebody know we love them, no matter what their emotions may be? Isn't that what we want when we're deep in it?

Somebody can only seek help when they are ready for it, when they initiate and get in the driver's seat for their wellness. Through connection, we provide and get provided a safe place where we can unload our pain, honor circumstances, and begin to heal. Connection is a key ingredient to healing others and ourselves, and it can't happen with judgment around. By noticing and sitting with our preconceived notions and beliefs, we add love into the mix. By judging others or ourselves, we put a barrier between us. We dig a gulf. We lock doors.

I will take things a step further and bring up a touchy subject, so please consider yourself warned: the full body autonomy and freedom of choice to commit suicide.

There is so much stigma around somebody who talks about wanting to die. How we handle it online, on social media, and in the world only pours the gasoline of disconnection on an already disconnected individual. I will never understand why we condemn suicide. It makes people fear speaking about it. It makes people ashamed of how they feel when we really want to encourage them to share by hearing what they say and responding with connection. The catastrophic response we've practiced as a society only catapults us further into a world that insists we only show the shiny life, that we pretend, that we continue to force a false sense of reality down one another's throats, which only makes everybody feel worse.

This is a dooming cycle. Everything, and I mean every single thing, can be a starting point for connection. Even talk of suicide. It may save somebody's life to discuss it, to think about dying differently. If someone wants to die, when someone wants to die, is not actually any of our business. I believe it's our job to remain in connection, to show up in a nonjudgmental way and hopefully that will be enough to help another person see it's not hopeless. Yet if they decide to go through with it, who am I to say that I understand enough about their circumstances that it wasn't their best choice? Who am I to be an expert on another's life or death?

It is my privilege to know somebody while they are alive and to connect with them. How they spend their time on earth, how they speak about it, about themself and others, that's also not my business. I'm not discounting the feelings somebody bears if they're suffering or if they've lost someone to suicide. I will never discredit pain. What I am saying is that someone who attempts suicide or succeeds at ending their life is in agony, just as somebody suffering from a physical illness is in agony. Don't we all have a right to live how we want to live...or not? Do we want to defend body autonomy or just sometimes?

I once felt so shame around how I grieved my father. The only way I got through that time was to notice and not condemn myself. It was observing that allowed the honest bereavement, and the connection with him wherever he was in whatever unearthly plane. From this mental space, I learned the tools to reparent myself. I gave myself the time to grieve the way I do, and to consider that no two episodes of grief need to look alike for them to be valid. Months later, I saw a friend lose his father and seem fine in it, yet shortly after that, when he lost his dog, he was bedridden with mourning. My initial reaction to this was admittedly to judge him – How can he be so sad over losing an animal and not a human? It was only when I saw and looked through a humble lens I heard myself say, Who am I to judge how someone grieves? Who am I to judge the way anyone processes their pain? There are no "shoulds" and "coulds." I can extend this to him because I'd given it to myself, I'd embodied it.

A gentle outlook towards ourselves and others is often connection's starting line. Judgement is almost always a cover for fear. It predicates on the fact that I might be doing it wrong, or else you are. It is such a scared way to live. When we notice what is there and mute the judgmental voice, we don't pretend it away. We merely decide there is no wrong or right way to mourn, or live, or die. So we mute what isn't true and can never be true. We thank our judgment for trying to protect us and then kindly ask it to quiet down. And though we should allow others to make their own decisions and not take away someone's rights by forcing them to go against their will, there is one place where we must step in, not from a judgmental stance but from a loving one and that is if somebody is harming another person. Somebody else's body is not yours to decide what to do with.

As imperfect as it is, we must decide upon whatever is safer for all individuals involved and society. One person's individual rights cannot take away a group's collective rights. A person has the authority to choose to be homeless, unmedicated even if wish it, to do drugs and abuse their body. But they do not have the authority to devalue or harm others or the communities we share. I very much value our legal system, which guarantees our basic freedoms and lets us make our own choices. The desire to restrict human rights gets dicey fast, though.

We may begin to wonder: Where are the lines? What about when the lines move? Judgement seeks lines. It seeks absolutes. Observation allows us not to abandon those who are sick or making poor decisions rather to continue letting them know we are here, even if we do not support their decisions. It is never complete rejection if we are coming from connection. We can remain kind and respectful, continue to stand for basic dignity, and continue to offer out our hand – using it to stop somebody only if they interfere with other's safety and freedoms.

Question for You

Please reflect on this conversation. Is there somewhere you may lay down your judgment, stay connected, and observe a person despite the situation they are in? Is it possible to hold space without melding into one another, to connect rather than direct, disinfect, or inject ourselves into somebody whose shoes we have never walked in? Maybe we should all take off our shoes and move around barefoot; maybe that is the way for judgment to disassemble so we can share this life.

Have you ever stared at toes for a while? How vulnerable they are, how quirky, how weird? We all have them. We are all the same.

There can be much more room for observation and less for arbitration. Connection through the souls of our feet.

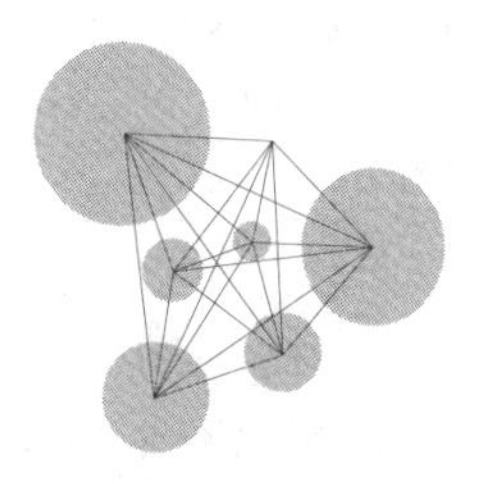

Conversation Thirty: From Insecurity to Resilience

Gandhi famously said, "A small body of determined spirits fired by an unquenchable faith in their mission can alter the course of history." Additionally, there is a quote in Judaism that has had a huge impact on me, which I mentioned in Conversation Fifteen: "Even if a knife is pointed at your neck, do not give up hope." What do these two quotes have in common? Resilience.

I have met people who have faced severe sickness, imminent financial ruin, struggles with their children, and severe trauma. But due to perseverance based in faith or positive thinking, these people have overcome life's obstacles. Maybe they cannot remove a problem, but they always ended up better off than anybody who gave up hope would have been. They never cashed in their determined spirits. Fear doesn't move us far. It embodies insecurity and it slows us down both when surviving and connecting. I want to clarify that fear is a normal and natural response, but staying in it past its due date is not. That is an option.

Countless studies have proven that when a person insists on a healing attitude, it helps them beat cancer. The power of resilience is a remarkable embodiment, especially when it happens in the face of cards stacked against us. How do we not retreat, though? How do we stand and have faith despite adversity? How can we build a sense of security in ourselves, and then use it to help others battling for their lives? We connect. We connect to our resilience, to our hope, and to others who have gone before us. We fan the flames of connection along the journey that builds resilience.

A huge part of my uncertainty derives from the fact that we never know what the future will bring. The odds are, it can bring something amazing things as likely as it can bring something terrible. Both possibilities are real so we must never be so uncertain that we live a life of gloom when there is no reason to be gloomy. Connection to what is actually going well is necessary for a happy, fulfilling life. And if we can master that, we can bolster ourselves so that when there is actually reason to be gloomy, we have an accumulation of happiness in our energetic accounts to lean on as we get through it. This gives us the belief that we can get through something. And if the mind believes it, often so it will be. I can't guarantee that will be the case, but I can bet that if the mind doesn't believe, it definitely won't be possible.

What I have learned is that change is scary and that our fears have information about trauma triggers for each of us. That's great news! It's a highlighter showing us what we must continue working on so we can connect to others, to ourselves, and to living. It nudges us to look back and reflect on all we've already surmounted.

Insecurity is like a monster that feeds on itself. There isn't anything we can do to quench its hunger because anything we can do is an illusion. There is no certainty. There is only change and the decision to be resilient in it, to believe we can be okay. In the 9th Step of the 12 Step program we are tasked to make amends wherever possible, unless to do so would injure others. This means upholding honesty but also, when in doubt, leave it out. Saying something so you can feel better or to assuage your guilt is not making amends. That would be for you, not for them. Likewise, resilience isn't about reminding people how hard life is or how much things suck. We can acknowledge someone's plight and hold hope for a better vision with them. We can be truthful while also making sure we always get their back, pointing towards their ability to bounce back.

I like to look people in the eye when they're speaking to let them know that I hear them. I do not lie or patronize them and promise everything will improve, yet I can promise them they need not go through this time alone and that enduring is probable. I tell them I will be right by their side because that is the truth. Please find a circle of gentle bodies that you can lean on when your resilience falters. Together you will tune each other like tuning forks do to the same sound that keeps us standing, so nobody has to fall. Loneliness is one of the major ills of today's society. Its baby is insecurity because to feel alone is to feel unloved and unlovable. Sometimes, letting a person know that you are there, embodying a listening ear, is enough to give them the buoyancy they need not to drown. They will be able to do it back for you. This is connection at its highest level – the kind that elevates us and catches us. This is how we keep hope alive and honor the determined spirits that are the ones who change the course of history.

Question for You

Here's an exercise for us to try together. Think of how you feel when things are good. Write down a list of words, what you think about, everything that comes to you about how you feel when things are going well. By tapping into this reservoir of ease, gratitude, and joy when it's available to you, you create a map for yourself of where to turn when things are harder. This is your resilience stockpile, a map of faith muscles you can flex and build by continuing to notice, breathe, pray, meditate, and converse with yourself about how good things can feel.

Resilience is more possible from a glass–is–half–full outlook, and trust me, as somebody who can see the glass as empty even when it's brimming, I know this can be tough. We must strive to feel in our bodies when things are wonderful because worry steals life from us. It steals our connections. It steals our ability to be resilient by keeping us paranoid instead. Especially when there's no need to worry. This practice helps me remember that I have the tools in me because there is always a time when things are going better. This practice helps me get out of living as if the other shoe is about to drop, constantly distrusting times of wellness when instead I can draw from those times the strength I will need to use to endure when life takes a turn.

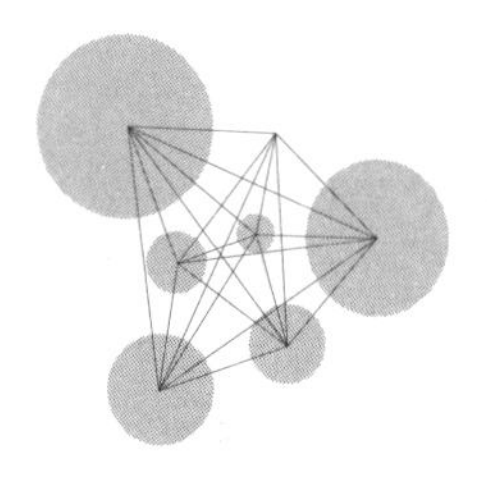

Conversation Thirty–One: From Symptoms to Causes

People keep getting sick. People are tired. People are in a bad mood. People wake up in night sweats. People can't sleep through the night. People feel like they don't have enough money, no matter how hard they try. People are bloated, jealous, drinking too much, eating too much, fantasizing too much or screaming at their children too much. People might be missing something but don't know what, and they fill that missing with everything they can get their hands on because the symptoms hurt. The lowness and the dimness and the loneliness and the unsettled buzz all hurt. They distract people in their blinding pain. They make people think they are the problem. They make people reach for another cigarette or guru or scapegoat.

Symptoms are side effects of something else. They're obvious and chaotic and in our faces, but symptoms are not the problem, the root cause, the issue, or the core of pain. If we want to be connected, for real, and in a way that means something to us, we have to strive to look around the symptoms, look behind the signs, look underneath the calls for help, and listen for the sound of something falling off a cliff. For the real center of gravity crashing. It might be a long way down, full of winds and fears nobody and nothing will catch us. It might be the thud of something landing broken in pieces. Then, after, it's just silence.

The causes are the invisible, buried under the rubble, searing wounds that require our attention to embody our true souls, the aliveness in us that makes us worthy of bonding to. Nothing else will ever do. We're moving air around until we get to the source of what ails us. Whether it be a traumatic event, a mental health challenge, a loss, a self–image issue, or one of the many other reasons we reach for a way to cope and numb out, causing us to then have symptoms, going right into the fire is the only way to actually heal.

In this hyper–technologically connected yet super disconnected world, we only see what people want us to see. Social media is a land where we only showcase perfection, glossy looks, stuff to brag about, and the assurance that our life is the absolute best, so why isn't yours? We know this isn't real, but it doesn't stop us from feeling bad about ourselves. And in this climate, where that is the norm and constantly shoved down our faces, where the way to "connect more" is based on a grossly disconnecting fountain, it can feel virtually impossible to find our people. The Internet is a fake, superficial void for the most part to attract one's tribe because to find and create the connected community we seek, we must be seen in all our glory and sorrow.

Going to meetings saved my life. Sharing my symptoms and hearing how common they were in the flesh with others. I learned I was not unique. What that did was give me a one–way ticket to what was going on, the cause of the boring, unoriginal symptoms, what lay at the base of my being, all the reasons I ate and drank and drugged. All the reasons I felt so uncomfortable inside of my skin. Once I began to dig into that, I found my people easily. There were others, like me, who felt self–discomfort and who were working their buns off to escape it. We were learning how to navigate life a different way, learning how to love ourselves anyway.

By getting to the cause of our unease, I argue that we can also get richer insight into what we are passionate about. We find our interests best like this, by going towards the screams and cries, by running towards the dark corners. It will reveal to us what we are meant to do and be, what we can give, who we are, where our gifts lie, and where our insights can turn into compassion that can overlap and help others. I urge you not to wait until you feel so disconnected, so isolated, so mired in symptoms that the molehill you have to deal with actually become an aching, shaking mountain.

Trials, tribulations and tragedies have the potential to bring about our biggest insights and our best behaviors. It is often the great motivator to try to change our lives, to become better versions of ourselves, and to connect around us and within us. I constantly wait to be slapped in the face before I wake up. Unfortunately, I learn my best lessons through suffering. We don't have to do it that way. That doesn't have to be how it goes. I hope that you might read this and choose to excel, choose to be inspired, and choose not to have to struggle knee–deep in symptoms of clear inner anxiety, terror, guilt, shame or sorrow to move you into living the life you wish to—and deserve to—live.

When we honor all who have gone before us, we can study their stories, reflect on their causes, and find connections into our own. Yes, even the dead are available to connect with, and I'm not talking about Ouija boards and seances. I'm talking about loving and missing. I'm talking about understanding the causes for why they were the way they were, recognizing the symptoms that acted as stand–ins for the work they had to do, and then using their cautionary tales as an impetus to act on that which we continuously put off until tomorrow. It's not about pardoning those we have lost, known to us or not known to us, although an indirect benefit is often that we will. It's about grief to know what's going on, to learn for ourselves, shed what needs shedding, dance with Great Pain, and know we can thrive by avoiding any of it.

The difference between shame and guilt is that the message we take from shame is usually, "I am bad," while guilt offers us, "I have done something wrong." We shall note the distinction between being rotten or an action being rotten because when the action is rotten, we can make amends and course correct, yet when we think we're rotten, there is nothing we can do to correct that. In Judaism, one of the prayers said every morning states, "My God, the soul you placed in me is holy."

The exact wording is important; it's not *was* holy or *will be* holy, rather it *is* holy. This is specifically intended to teach us the distinction between shame and guilt. Shame wants to tell us that every day isn't a new day and that we don't have a choice because we're horrible, with all of our defects and with no ability to change, which can be a cause resulting in so many unhealthy symptoms because we accept the lie the mind whips into us. Guilt shows up and says, "You see that you are holy today, you are good, and you are worthy just because you exist. Although it is still important that you think about the actions that you have done wrong, use that to motivate you so you can clean things up to the best of your ability and stop stewing in them or letting them define you."

Such is the human condition that we would tell ourselves, "We are bad, and we might as well not try to be better" if not for God's mercy. We will make it about shame instead of guilt if not for God. However, when connected with God, when we look to our core and not to the indications that a problem distract us from diving into the core, we can learn of wrong behavior, regret it, and change without telling ourselves that we are inherently wrong and need to change our being. There is nothing inherently bad about any of us. I believe that. It's our actions that may need to change, and when we change them, we can combat shame and begin to connect to this great miracle of living.

What I'm being longwinded about is this: Your cause is not you. Do not fear it. You are a good soul. You are a golden soul. You are a soul of God. Love yourself, love the cause, and watch the symptoms that haunt you melt away.

Question for You

What are the symptoms in your life that plague you most? Is it the way you eat fast and until you're too full, so that you don't even notice or taste the food? Is it smoking cigarettes? Is it your temper, your quickness to judge? Your defects are not you. They are symptoms of something else, and I'd like to invite you to wonder what that might be.

To take these above examples, when we eat too much and too fast, we might be using food to leave ourselves, to leave our lives. Here, food is the symptom, but the cause is what we're not looking at, the real thing, the reasons we want to leave. We smoke to avoid boredom or anxiety, but cigarettes, as a symptomatic response, lose hold faster if we stay with why we're bored or anxious and deal with that. Our anger and judgments too – they are covers for pain, fear, and even loneliness.

Please set down the dazzling warning signs for a moment, and all they entail, and all they enrapture. And consider instead what might be causing them. That part of you needs your love the most.

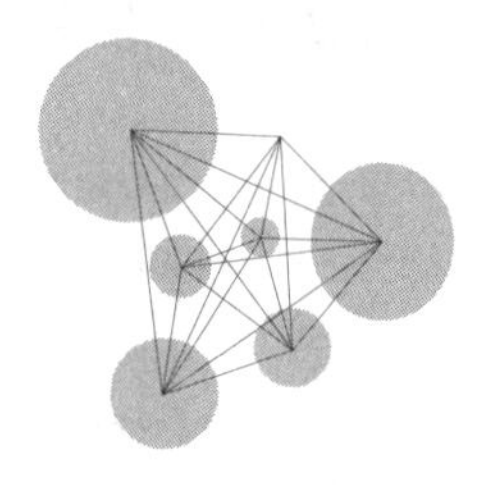

Conversation Thirty–Two: From Vigilance to Tenderness

Forgiveness demands introspection. The way to tenderness is in this lane. In most religions, there is time dedicated to doing a deep dive into the past year to clear resentments and make amends. To forgive and let go of any ill will we are carrying for others, and to ask for forgiveness too, admitting our wrongs. We can then plan for the next year, and create space for blessings, for evolving, for more love. In the 12 steps, there are these steps as well.

This process is the soil of connection, and it's called forgiveness. Both as energy going out from us and coming in towards us, forgiving enrichens and nourishes everything it grows in and that grows in it. Forgiveness of self must be included, as self–hatred occupies way too much of our brain capacity, making it difficult for us to see, let alone allow, the good.

Once, I was at a communications workshop in Barbados and was asked, “What was the most pivotal moment in your life?” To which my partner, a young woman, replied: “It was the day I went to my perpetrator’s house and told him I won’t forget what happened, but that I forgave him. I will no longer allow him to live rent–free in my head.”

Please know I’m not suggesting anybody forgive on my timeline or even at all. It’s an individual choice, one instance at a time. I am simply sharing how forgiveness relieved this woman of the huge burden she was lugging around, not only of the trauma that had been done to her but of the event inside herself that the trauma had caused. The bitterness and pain it fueled, which took energy away from other areas in her life, which made her more vigilant than she wanted to be in order to live connected and free. In my life, whenever I have forgiven, it has released a huge burden from me, a huge paranoia, and a huge responsibility. To be exonerated is an amazing feeling of grace. The only thing I’ve found that beats it is to be the one doing the pardoning. When forgiveness stirs inside of me, a willingness to let go, that is as close to God as I ever get.

An idea I try to live by is that it’s not enough to get rid of anger, I must also be a vessel for grace. I must take the actions inside of *me* to forgive *you* without waiting for you to forgive me. This makes everyone, even the people who have wronged us, a gift in our lives. This makes us all deeply connected because we are all human, we are all flawed, and we are all making mistakes. It also lets us be one another’s opportunities for the miracle that is mercy, something we can pray for and become ready for, but not rush or demand. We wait for forgiveness to descend upon us, and it does. It is a gift from the Above we are connected to, clearing us inside, lifting the weight in us, and reducing our load so we can move on in life more joyfully and easily.

I'm reminded of a story of two couples who couldn't have children. Both couples went to a clergyman for a blessing to have children. The following year, one couple came back to thank the clergyman, reporting it worked, but the other came back to ask why the blessing had not come true for them. The clergyman brought both couples into a room together and asked the one whose blessing came true to share what they did after they left their meeting the previous year. The couple said, "We rejoiced, celebrated, saved money, and prepared for our blessing!" Then, the second couple was asked what they did, to which they replied, "We continued to pray and wait. It wasn't happening."

The moral of the story—as the clergyman summed up to both in the room—is that when a blessing will not come true, it is much harder for it to be possible. Tenderness is like that. Tenderness connects us to the it–already–happened feeling of joy and gratitude and celebration, and then one of two things manifests: the connection strengthens like we expected it to, and it manifests, or it doesn't, but we're happier anyway. We can't lose. We make a situation for ourselves where we cannot lose this way, where we are loved, and everything and anything is proof of that. By being so vigilant like the couple who waited for the prayer to be answered, they were emitting to the Universe and to themselves an energy of disembodiment to the tune of, "What if it doesn't happen? It's not going to happen. Keep watching. See, it didn't happen!" Part of a blessing, of forgiving, of receiving, of connecting is believing that we are a vessel for what we seek. Then and only then can what we seek meet us. Then and only then can the blessing come true.

Touchy subject, but I will go there. Because if I'm not being real with you then am I even connecting as fully as I can to you, Dear Reader? I want to talk about cancel culture. I want to acknowledge that cancel culture was born out of a much–needed response to finally rid society of hate, racism, and bigotry so we can, for once and for all, begin to treat people fairly. Unfortunately, we have stopped giving people the benefit of the doubt, and we have forgotten about or ignored due process. We live in a gotcha environment where many are looking to call somebody out and bring them down. We're vigilant and waiting to be proved right that another is wrong, instead of noticing opportunities to soften, teach, and forgive.

This is the most disconnecting behavior we can practice. How and why would this inspire or motivate others to respect those who deserve to be respected and haven't historically been given fair treatment? I can't understand. I believe if we would simply take a different approach and assume the best in others, try to teach and model so we can connect first, then we can achieve the goals cancel–culture set out to reach. By waiting to pounce on others and guardedly waiting for them to mess up as if that's the prize, well, sorry to say, but it's doing more harm than good. Being wary of each other prevents us from binding to one another, from understanding one another with compassion, and from making the changes we need to make inside so everybody is treated well outside.

It's happened to me. I've said a joke in poor taste and been told I would be cancelled, been yelled at, been verbally slain for it as if I haven't lived for decades fighting for justice for all or doing what I needed to do to become an ally. I have felt terrible that I said something to upset or offend somebody and did everything I could to repair my mistake and learn more.

Thankfully when this happened I was eventually granted grace. I was handled as if I could make a mistake, spoken to as if I was a good person who wanted to do better because I am. And it made all the difference in the world to be dealt with through the lens of forgiveness. It encouraged a deeper connection in me and between us, and it revved me up to advocate harder for those I could support.

When we live vigilantly in a pre–angry state before something has even happened because we're already convinced it will, we live with what's called a cognitive bias. And it's hard for someone to prove us wrong when we live like that, or get through to us, or connect with us. Because from this seat we will only see what we want to see. This does not serve us in evolving, in progress, or in unifying. To trust people, to correct and redirect, to forgive, to assume the best in others and treat them in a way that helps them rise to a higher standard, this is how we encourage people to *want* to stand up for others, to want to be careful and fair. This is true equality; I'm not totally right, and you are not totally right either. Both of us affect each other and growing together, biases set down and set aside so we need not live waiting to break one another. We're too busy looking out for each other's tender parts, giving each other the benefit of the doubt, and living ready to love our fellows. This is what connection feels like.

Question for You

Jot down things you wish you could say and how you can say them better, how you would, if people were supporting you instead of tearing you down. Write down the things you wish you could effect change around, language you would like to help others improve and be known to yourself within your truth, but also through the expansion of your sympathy.

This should be the culture we aim for.

Everything we aspire to starts with an idea. Write it down. In time, as we stay connected to this dream, it will be brought to life.

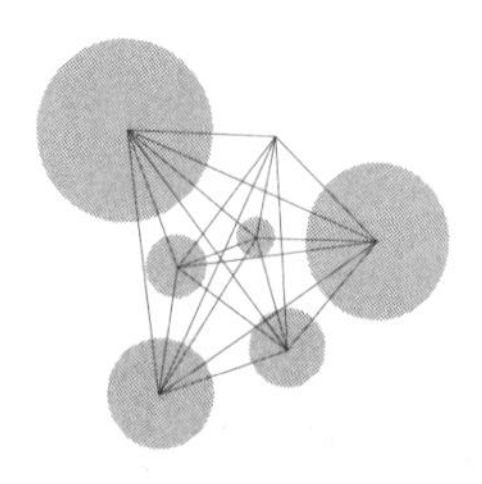

Conversation Thirty–Three: From Worry to Fun

My fears and uncertainties have brought me closer to those unfortunate people suffering through unexpected tragedies. I understand what it feels like to live in a constant state of doubt and concern, most familiar with the edges of worry and the safety it promises to offer. Worrying about something has never brought me strategies or remedies, though; it has only drained me of having a good time.

Living a life arranged around and because of connection means having some faith. In my highest self, in a Higher Power, in the higher states of consciousness from others, in something more than me. When I embody this faith, I can begin to practice being okay with not knowing what the greater picture is, not knowing where the car God is driving is taking me. I just don't know. We don't know everything, or often anything, and worrying about that doesn't change it. The pandemic revealed to us how much we cling to the illusion that we are in control. All we can do, the choice we always have, is to enjoy the road trip, metaphorically speaking. Look out the window, hear the music, and have fun. That is our birthright.

FOMO, or fear of missing out, is a predator's poison. It is a byproduct of social media, and its presence in our lives predicates how much we'll use our Smartphones. Think of that – the people who invented most of the online world rely on you to feel left out, like you need to catch up, behind and worried, as if the answer of the world may be in the next post, so you can't dare miss it. This concern with what others think and do makes them a lot of money. And it causes us equal suffering. It is a disconnected, distracted, and destructive way to live, overly focused on what is happening in rooms you're not even a part of. It's a human tendency run rampant, turned up all the way, and for what? For profit.

But again, if we will redirect our focus on having fun in our lives, our real, happening–now lives! This is how we trump FOMO, this is how we reengage in a world that values presence over performance. Because underneath FOMO or produced social media posts is a feeling of supreme loneliness rooted in our inability to show our real selves, coupled with the acknowledgment that other people are also not showing their real selves. It's phoniness and fakeness squared, and nothing is more detaching or severing to us than living a lie. It requires us to put on a show for others, to keep testing out what makes them like us, which is basically being concerned with what others think of us as if we have to earn it all the time. It's codependency and false worship. Do you see how groundbreaking having a good time in your life can be, what it is combatting?! It is combatting the addiction social media has birthed.

Fear of missing out causes us to be unable to stake a flag in the ground because we are constantly afraid of what may be, or wondering if the flag we chose was wrong, or distractedly looking over there to another ground to see if it's better or if we shall quickly move over to it. This activates self–doubt, paralysis, and depression. This leads to a struggle to put a call out into the universe about who we are and what we do, something like, "Hi, this is me, and this is my purpose, my passion!" which is what will bring your community to you and drive you towards those right for you. But if we're all experiencing FOMO and trapped in it, we're cooking ten pots at the same time, driven by fear of being wrong, distrusting ourselves and then putting nothing in the ground. No call. No flag. No you. How will we ever find our people and our connections this way? Then we look at the evidence of not having that as proof we suck. That something is wrong with us. Someone out there or some post can fix it so we can't miss it! What a vicious cycle.

Nothing is wrong with any of us. If only we put having fun first, if only we were honest about where we wanted to play today, we will end up in a land with a flag, the call beaming long and strong and our circle widening. We will belong to ourselves and then to others. It must come from us, not from outside. Our good time must be louder and prouder than anybody else's good time.

If reading that makes you uncomfortable and squirmy, or has you shaking your head at me, or if you immediately want to scream about how I'm selfish and an individualist, that's alright. I can hold space and compassion for you, and we can let that be here with us. May I ask you to be willing, or to pray for the willingness to be willing, to consider that you have bought into a story that doesn't serve you? How does keeping yourself away from having a good time and enjoying life do anything for you, or for anybody? How does it add to collective liberation or improve the world for you to feel badly? How does being miserable, agitated, and bothered solve problems or bring you the sonic openings of insight that could flow your way if you felt well enough to receive them? Fretting blocks access. Fretting blocks downloads. Fretting blocks the perhaps small, maybe unsexy, maybe mundane acts we can take day to day to be good to ourselves and be good to others. This is the stitch of significant connection – that good feeling fun we can both sew and be woven by if we let ourselves.

I'm reminded of a story I heard in early recovery at an Alcoholics Anonymous meeting about a man walking into a room worried about how people will receive him. And he was told that he was about to walk into a room full of self-centered people who were way too busy thinking about themselves to think about him! I chuckled at that. Because it's true. Nobody is thinking of us, we're all thinking of ourselves! Our head can be our own worst enemy. Our fears of others' opinions of us and of what we might be missing out on are offshoots of the self-centered, insecure parts of our brains. The truth is it's not our business what others think of us, and it doesn't really matter, but what we think of ourselves actually counts a lot. FOMO mugs us daily of that lesson. It prevents us from seeking our approval, which is the only one we need. We can't let it.

To some extent, if we're paying attention in the world today, we all have a little FOMO because our current world is designed to unearth it consistently. All we are missing out on when we play into it and become pawns of it is what we are doing right now. The present moment is what's real. It's where the fun and the good feeling are. It's where loneliness and isolation give way to clarity and peace of mind. As much as you can and however you can, stop the worrying. Trust you. Trust you can't miss anything that is for you. Embody a dedication to enjoying your destiny by keeping your eyes on your plate. Nobody else's destiny is yours, and thankfully, yours is no one else's.

Question for You

Here's an exercise: settle in with prayer or meditation, and then when you're ready, list all the things you will do to bring yourself joy today. In black and white, write it down. How do you have a good time? What makes you feel good? This is not silly! This is not luxurious or irresponsible. This is a blueprint for connection. Because God wants us to feel good, our souls want to feel good, and the way we attract connection to others happens fastest and smoothest when we feel good. If it's hard to make this list, if you struggle to come up with what to write down...that's great information. It shows you how much this muscle needs to build, how far away you may have come from seeking play in your life for fun or from even tending to your inner voice telling you what you like. Yet fun is a divine and revolutionary act. It is both.

We don't see enough examples of this that depict to us how fun is sticking it to the man, how fun is giddy time with Source, playing in our fateful sandbox. This is often the medicine I need most in order to deal with instability, unpredictability, and uncertainty. This is commonly the way I can best get around worry, or at least quiet my concerns down, stop scratching the itch – by focusing instead on following one question, one moment at a time: *What will make me feel good right now?*

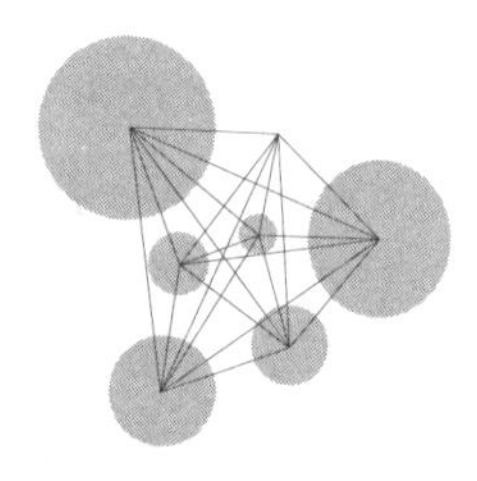

Conversation Thirty–Four: From Pain to Opportunity

Sometimes, it seems like bad things happen to good people, and good things happen to bad people. We can't make sense of it. Boy, does it cause us pain. Because when we look at the world through this perspective, nothing feels just or often even worth it. People in the most difficult socioeconomic situations are always affected the most severely, which never seems fair or purposeful. So how can we regard what hurts so bad to witness and especially to live through? How can we make meaning out of it that might serve us instead of bring us down?

The only ray of hope I have discovered along the way is to consider every pain point as an opportunity despite its nature. If we get caught up in self–pity, in my circumstance is the worst, in martyrdom, we will struggle to transform any challenge into something useful that can connect us to others. "Why me?" can be replaced by "What's the insight here?" Because we are spiritual beings have a human experience, and nobody ever said it would be fabulous every moment of the journey. We have no right to any less pain than another person. We have the right to sit in the muck and then, when we're ready, refurbish it into something meaningful.

One thing I know for sure is that my greatest lessons have not come during happy times or even fair times. It's usually during trials of intense hardship I grow and reach out and reach up, which leads to connections being made both outside of me with others but also inside of my brain. As in new synapses being formed, new pathways, new mental circuitry to see me through and change my life. It's inside life that changes first; that's what I'm getting at. And then the outside shifts from there. How smart Higher Power is to design us that way, for if we changed outside first, we wouldn't need the mental filters, the eyes and ears, or even the recognition of our hearts to understand our new reality.

Adversity as harshness often has equal–in–measure qualities of tranquility and love. There is the storm, and there is after the storm. There is even before the storm, but we don't know what that is or why it matters until after a storm happens. In that way, a storm comes to shed light. To enlighten us. We do not have control over what hurts us and when it will come, yet we always have control over how we see it working for us...or not. How we see it unraveling what was hidden before the hardships came.

There's a reason we talk about rock bottom in recovery.

The pain often has to get that grave, that grotesque, that we are moved to do something. To embody a spirit that looks for prospects despite any inkling that there is even hope is to live connected to a future that hasn't even happened yet. But we can see it. We can hold to it. We can strive for it. We can make it our mission to tend to that vision and myopically focus on any steps, big or small, and any opportunities which will get us to it. This is how we make life–long changes for our benefit and evolution.

"No pain, no gain," we've heard it said a thousand times before. Where is the rest of the quote? Where is the lesson on connection that this saying misses out on? Which is to say that by touching our pain and sitting with our grief, we can touch others. We can connect with others. We can compassionately feel others' pain as our own.

Too often a word like "opportunity" is turned into a bad word, a capitalist idea, a selfish end that is inherently evil. But why? Why can't we want for ourselves and strive and attain? Why are those things made to be bad? Why can't we see the gold at the end of a dark rainbow and let ourselves dance in it? Why can't we do that for others? It is this polarized, pitting against one another—"us versus them" or "selfish versus unselfish" or "oppressor versus oppressed" that flattens people, that steals our three–dimensional–ness, and that frankly keeps people in cycles of stuck pain. Because nobody wants to choose to be "them" or "selfish" or "oppressive," and so we choose to give away our dreams and goals, our joy and even our potential to stay safe in the pain camp. Then nobody gets ahead, and nobody gets mad. And we will never meet opportunities to connect with all that life can be, and we will never move onward.

We fear moving away from the throbbing to morph it into the break we've been searching for, that is a match for us. We fear connecting to having more, being proud of it, being grateful for it by celebrating it, and so we fail to see that if we live with limitations about what ails us, we cannot offer much to others. We can suffer together, and we choose it to thrive alone. It need not be this way where we cannot be for ourselves or others. Empathy for an "opposite side" comes from empathy for oneself. To have empathy, we must experience the full scope of our emotions, both the dark and the light, the bad and the good, and allow a perspective that having and wanting are okay.

If it would threaten the status quo and rock the boat, we will not move much from the position we're in, even if we feel we are held back the whole time we're there. Connection in its wildest, purest, most alive form takes us forward because we are real in the present. It heals the past because we are present. It syncs us up to every feeling, to sitting with the pain and not rushing through it, and to the idea that beyond the pain is a break in the clouds, where the sun shines to warm us, and we get to have it. Connection lets us move into the heat and appreciate and invite others to join us. It requires us to leave the pain behind us once we have woven it into something beautiful.

We're all shapeshifters because life is a changing force. We are not meant to run in place and tread water for fear we will be disliked. Whoever would dislike you for improving your life, they dislike you already because if someone wants to hate there are 100 available reasons to hate anybody. They don't need your permission to justify a belief they've been holding and dying to prove true. You cannot please them.

What matters is: *What is underneath that belief?* Who will they have to face? What will they have to deal with if they stopped critiquing you and looked at themselves? That is their work to do, and the greatest gift you can give them is the chance to do it. To sit with their pain. And because you've done so, because you have moved into the land of opportunities and have more for yourself, you can take their hand and let them know, *I've been there. I get it. You are not alone.*

This is the most marvelous opportunity. It requires courage. This is the biggest win that can ever come from your pain. To help another through theirs, when and if they're ready, by being the one on the other side. The identity they must lose as they dismember the attachment to the hurt story will become a gorgeous metamorphosis as they embody the person full of possibilities they can't wait to meet that's waiting for them. And because of a connection to you, they'll be able to do it, with you in a front–row seat cheering them on. This is a way we can improve the world for everybody.

Question for You

I'd like to invite you to think about a daily routine you can create to remind yourself how to look at the pain in your life. So we don't revert to the ways we were before the pain (aka before the storm), we shall consider what needs to shed and elevate, what the rawness of the pain might have to tell us and teach us. Where does it hurt? What would the hurt say if it could speak – if it got the pen or the microphone?

Maybe taking five minutes a day for your pain to take center stage would be good for your soul. Maybe having some cry time, or writing in a journal. The goal is to tend to yourself, to let it be intuitive and responsive, for the needs to change, but to commit to listening to the pain as an essential part of your voice that should not be rushed or silenced or rejected. The opportunity is right there, in giving it its importance.

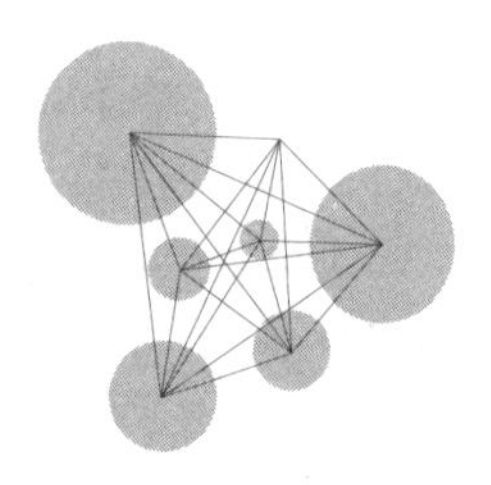

Conversation Thirty Five: From Power to Integrity

Recently, I was reading an article about power by Rabbi Jonathan Sacks. According to Sacks, power is a "zero–sum" concept that states if I give something up, I have less. This notion is forced on others and results in jealousy and envy. Whenever you have power, somebody will exist, aiming to dethrone you, to be better, to take away from you so they can have more. Because power is finite—there is only so much of it. When one loses power, someone else is gaining power, and vice versa. We must battle for it; it is not lasting, and for the most part, we don't look up to people with power, or if we do, it's not because of their power. It's usually because of their skill, talent, or charisma. And we want to take it all from them.

Integrity is a multiplier. I don't need you to have it for me; I only need to be true. There's more than enough, an infinite amount, and so there's nothing to fight for. Me having integrity takes nothing away from you having integrity. We carry our integrity with us wherever we go and are loved for it, and because it is expansive, it inspires others, and it generates goodwill in others and from others. Additionally, the more we are in integrity, the more it grows, and so its uprightness can be an everlasting attribute that makes us reliable.

Who doesn't want to connect with somebody reliable?

Hands down, parenting has to be the most arduous job a human can do. We don't have a guidebook; it moves at its own pace, and no matter what we do or how hard we try, we inevitably make mistakes. Parenting is a forward–focused activity that can feel thankless as it's all about the child, but it is also a backwards–intensive pursuit that makes you reflect on your childhood, what you got from your parents, and that makes it about you. Too often, we can't look at our wounds, so we enforce what we demand on our kids. Too often, parents use power dynamics to force their children to do what they want them to do instead of using integrity. One teaches children how to go out in the world and reach for power; the other teaches children how to focus on honor. One breeds disconnection and competition, the other fosters closeness and mutual respect.

Look, I can't tell you how to parent. I'm not a parenting expert and I am still figuring the job out. When we embody a principle, we influence others with it. The world I see today, the kids I see today, man, their homes must be brimming with power struggles. Because integrity is faltering our youth, and it's dragging us down a steady decline.

The single most important things I can do for my children is to pay attention and let them know that they are important and to be a father to them of morals and decency because kids learn by what we do so much more than what we say. Day after day, we show our children how to be. We model to them what to do by being it with them, in front. That's the role. That's the responsibility. Behaving as a person who leads with integrity and does not concern myself with power is good for me but also good for my children. I hope that it produces individuals who know how to connect, who know how to uphold who they are, and who do not engage in the power struggles that steer participants into modes of domination, supremacy, and might. Power may feel like protection, it may feel like you're the big cheese, but it will not produce connection. It is antithetical to dignity because to keep power, one must throw decency out the window if that's what it takes.

But if we value what we say by being it, our kids will listen and value what we say, too. They will go out into the world with this internal center point that doesn't concern itself with false ideas about contentment because they will know true contentment comes from who you are, how you are, day in and day out, especially around the people you love. Power is an imposition. It blocks explanation and freedom and will fail in forming connection. I will never trade in my relationship with my kids and loved ones for a sense of authority or to hoard the privileges that could someday be taken away from me.

If something can be taken away, it was never ours. Only what is ours can never be taken. Integrity comes from within. Living this way is living with value, and it can be felt by others. People will be so much more interested in what we are sharing if we show them that what they share is valuable, too, which is impossible if all we're striving for is power over them.

Throughout history, at numerous times, horrendous acts have been condoned in the name of power. This is how the connection of society at large begins to erode and, if we're not careful, is erased. This is the greatest price a country can pay. The collective efforts of a nation, the peace, pride, and patriotism cultivated by being connected under a shared country are the backbone of what it means to be strong and successful. Without it, we are risking everything at the expense of mayhem and anarchy. Because it's the connections between neighbors and citizens, constituents and those appreciating the values their country offers them, that ultimately decide how great of a place it is to live. We cannot fall for power plays between us, within a homeland. We can protest, argue, insist on checks and balances, and fight for our people, but with integrity so that unity is never compromised.

I have been to the concentration camps. We must never forget the atrocities. They stand for how evil power can be. Many times I have wanted to seek counsel from people who proclaim to have special abilities. Why not consider that some people have a higher connection to Source or are more plugged in and intuitive? A fellow rabbi told me we shouldn't seek answers about the future; we should only seek guidance and advice on how to behave our best now.

I've sat in contemplation many times throughout my life to try and find predictions, explanations, some way to make sense. I've tried to assure myself that another Hitler will never rise to power. Anybody from a group that's been persecuted will understand what I mean here, will comprehend the desperate desire for guaranteed safety. We live with scars on our souls of how our people suffered and died under the formidable entities that hated us. Another rabbi told me that prophecies and future telling are usually a warning of what will happen if we don't change our ways *now*. We still have a chance to live with integrity if we connect because of integrity. If we trade *more for me* for a better life *for all.*

We've overcomplicated things because of power. It shouldn't be that difficult for each of us to be the best version of ourselves and support others in doing the same. It shouldn't be impossible to live in harmony and with honor. I know I can be idealistic and that what I am describing above does not come easy for everyone nor all the time. I realize that wars have been fought for and against such notions. What I am saying is that we should never take a homeland for granted. To acknowledge that we're in the same boat as others is to say, "Here, here is some of my power. Or better yet, let's live with integrity together instead."

That is the world I want to wake up to.

Question for You

The real question for me then is, how can we come from a place where integrity is what we're working for, rather than power we can wield? This isn't something we will learn from the world, as integrity is not valued over power in most places. This is something we have to strive to model and represent in our homes, with our families and with our children.

I invite you now to set a timer and put your pen to paper. Free write about integrity, without editing yourself and without trying to impress anybody. As distinct from authority, what does the word mean to you? Who do you see with integrity that you want to model? And once you come up with a name or a list of names, jot down some things those people do. How do they lead? Inspire? Love the world?

They say imitation is the highest form of flattery. So go on and flatter—copy those people. Copy what they do, even if it's one thing for one day. Adopt behaviors of integrity and be the person who chooses honor over power by intentionally setting out to act like one.

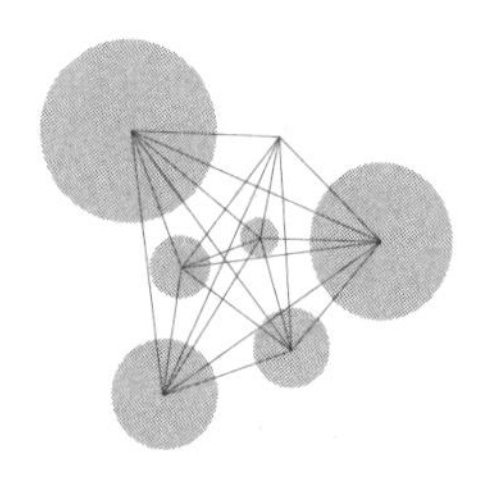

Conversation Thirty–Six: From Disconnection to Connection

A teacher named Ted taught me that life is a journey of falling in love with oneself. I have so often misconstrued what this means over the years, thinking that if I loved myself, I would become egotistical or stop seeking the counsel of others, among many other misbeliefs. So, I would resist the notion that I should be in love with myself.

There are millions of versions of what self–love might look like and millions of versions of why we're afraid to have it. Ted's idea was that loving ourselves fully is the point of our existence, and as generous for others as it is for ourselves. His point is also that each of us must define what self–love is for ourselves and bring down the lies that hold us back from going after it. It's in the going after it that we reach it – self–love is not some finish line we win in a race. It's earned in the doing, in the commitment to self. And I bet self–love is less likely to manifest without connection mixed into its recipe.

For most of my life, I thought love was you agreeing with me and unconditionally supporting me. I realize now that's not love; that's fandom. Love is when someone close to us will hold up a mirror and call us out lovingly if we're not behaving in a way that suits connection, or that steps on our known values. Love is when someone will take a risk for our benefit. Love is not offering an opinion, not imposing ourselves on others. Most of all, love is choosing each day – it is the decision to connect again. Love has a leadership quality to it. You can lead one another in love, and you can follow one another when the other leads. It's a sort of back and forth that prevents rips in the fabric that dresses what is between you.

In the Bible, Noah, who created the ark and saved his family and animals from the flood, which destroyed the world, was considered a great man. However, according to one interpretation of Rashi who was a 10th century scholar, had Noah lived in the generation of Abraham, he wouldn't have been considered the great man he was.

What it boils down to is leadership. When God told Noah he would destroy the world, Noah asked God to save his family. Yet, when God told Abraham he would destroy Sodom and Gomorrah, Abraham argued and negotiated with God to save everybody, not just his own family. Abraham pleaded with God, asking if fifty worthy people were worth rescuing, would God spare them all? And Abraham only conceded when he concluded that there weren't even ten worthy people in the city. Then there is Moses, who said to God when told he would destroy the world: "God, if you destroy the world, please destroy me too, as who am I without my people, who am I without my brothers and sisters." This is even higher leadership. This is connection. This is a definition for love.

We must be like Abraham, and if we're brave enough, even like Moses and lead everybody. For some of us, it'll be easier; we connect in our bones and our souls, and we feel we are one with all. For others, it feels distant, and it will take effort. That's okay, too. Yet, no matter what the case is, we shall keep striving. To keep showing solidarity, support, and speak up. Nurture our connections to live with devotion and remember that what happens to a single person happens to every one of us.

True faith, true spirituality, is like this as well. Religion should have an intellectual pursuit and a belief system. And to be open to allowing space for those who are dissimilar from us, despite their views, faith must also be an emotional pursuit. It's the connection between emotion and intellect, head and heart, that cultivates a deep knowing we can count on, even when we can't see or feel anything to be connected to even when we think we are not like that other person. We must decide to trust repeatedly that we're taken care of, despite whether proof of that comes in time or in hindsight, while also holding the interconnectedness between everybody.

After thirty–five chapters, you are well on your way to connection now as a lifestyle. Keep fighting for your right to feel it and to collect evidence of your wholeness as part of the whole world. When we grow complacent, we must remind one another within the circles of our communities. When we grow cynical, we must give each other room to sink to the bottom so we can push off the ocean floor and break through the surface to gasp for air. And then it hits us that every breath is connection. Every inhale and exhale is a new connection again.

There's nothing about you that is ever too flawed or broken for this to be true. In the 12 Steps, the 9th Step promise is: "No matter how far down the scale we have gone, we will see how our experience can benefit others." Inside out, outside in, up and down, from all directions and diagonals, you are doing the thing now; you are tapping in. I believe that wholeheartedly. It's as if I knew you before I wrote the first line of this book, as if I knew you were out there, I knew you could do it, and I knew we'd meet. And as someone who has been mistaken about so many things in my life, it feels so nice to be correct sometimes. You are the dream come true.

Question for You

How do we come to see the similarities between us instead of the differences? How do we hold the truth, no matter what, that we are all seeking the same things – safety and connection? It is reasonable for us to coexist and to live as one family, the human family.

Many years ago, my teacher Ted had me do an exercise, which I will pass along and ask you to do as well. Ted drew a scale on the floor, like a ruler of sorts, labeled one through ten. He asked me to stand on the spot where I identified myself, zero being the lowest and ten being the highest, as he questioned me: How was my mood? How did I feel about the people in my life? About my work? About my impact? You can play this with anyone you want and ask (and be asked) questions you want. The key was for me to acknowledge any difficult circumstances occurring as well as any sadness, to admit where my thinking was limited, and to identify my polarity, the light and darkness within me, the potential for both good and bad. As a physical activity, it let me experience empathy with the humanness in myself so I can extend it to others. We all feel this way.

Being seen as I did while doing this activity helped me find common ground with Ted and with humankind. Nobody is all right or all wrong, and often, the truest test of connection is whether we can make room for the differences within ourselves and between ourselves and others. Somebody whose language, ideas, religion, culture, customs, and values might be unlike mine, can I still recognize God in them and connect with the places we're both human? Embodying alternate points of view is a skill to be practiced and honed. Because for every person who thinks like a conservative (or fill in the blank), there's somebody beside them who thinks like a liberal (fill in the opposite blank).

It's all about you being comfortable and secure in who you are so you can stretch yourself enough to consider how the person on the opposite side of you might think. Because we are in a relationship with, and interrelated with, everything around us, both what is visible and what is not.

As an experiment, what if we felt that before we took the first bite of each meal or drink of water, as we interacted with the mailman or the neighbor walking the dog? What if we inserted a hundred moments in our days to experience and embody just how miraculously everything is woven together? I believe this will exalt even the simplest of tasks and lift us into the magic of transcendent connection.

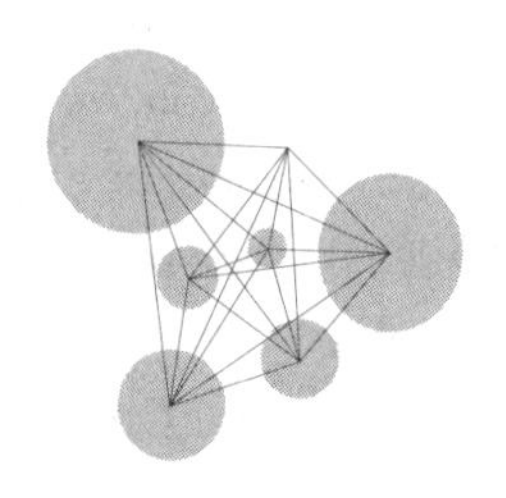

CONCLUSION

I have done a lot of forcing, both in business and personal matters. I have stayed in relationships for too long, ignoring the warning signs. I have remained in business partnerships without thinking them through, trying to shove them into working. I have convinced myself to be a man I wasn't and to behave in ways I loathed. This all led me to such intense frustration I couldn't see my way through it. I didn't know how I'd ever feel differently or better or connected in my body, in my life. It was all on me to build what I thought I wanted, but I did not know how, and I did not have the tools to create my house never mind keep it in order.

Fear controlled me and told me, what if this person thought this, what if this thing was the winning horse and I was wrong, what if I needed that! I knew how to search for something outside of myself to fill me up and give me shelter. Yet the faithful action began when I gave up. When things got that bad. When I had honest dialogues, and when I started to let go. When I stopped being complicit and practiced following my internal compass, which turned out to not only be alive but beating to its harmonious drum. This inner beat, this emission from a lighthouse, brought me back to myself.

You know what they say about hindsight...

While I place immense trust in my Higher Power and in a benevolent universe with a plan grander than anything I can imagine, I also take great ownership of the responsibility I have. The power of my thoughts and words, my actions and my energy. The capability to connect, to stand dry and warm under the asylum of connection all around me, which I have built and which has been built without me, too. We cannot micromanage or determine every variable in life, but we are incredible agents of change, causing it and receiving it. I hope the principles you've read along these pages keep you balanced and open, guided by your integrity and code, living a both/and existence that ushers in love from all directions.

Because then disconnection's deep dark cave where loneliness, depression, addiction, and desperation thrive can get demolished. A bridge can be built on one side. Or on both sides. There can be no division anymore, no need for the bridge, the bridge evaporates into a land of unification. It will turn into a home. Our home. We are our own homes. There was only ever home. We just didn't know it. We'd forgotten how to come home to ourselves.

Was connection ever easy and we've made it hard? It's probably been a multifaceted idea since the dawn of our time, trickier than we wished and always requiring our thinking and doing and saying and embodying. It does not matter if it's doable or difficult; what counts is that we live trying.

Life is a string of opportunities to try again. Connection is not for credit, for followers, to look good on an application, or for any external, agenda–based accomplishment. It is an individual journey to feel whole in a disconnected world. It is showing up for the world beyond yourself and only for yourself, body and mind and mostly, soul.

Hello. My soul is the one writing this book. It is emanating across these words. It is synching up with your soul, they are laughing, they are taking a walk, they are familiar to each other and new and noteworthy.

It's why I wrote this – to be connected to you. Pick up this book again whenever you doubt it or feel alone. I'm here, you're here, and we're in it together.

We are together.

Those three words, so small, can be so huge.

The shelter you are building, your shelter, you are doing it with your bare hands. With your beating heart. With your brilliant brain. With your soul. Standing underneath it and being protected and warmed there is an indescribable feeling. You can decorate your shelter as your sanctuary, however you see it, and spruce it up whenever you feel so inclined, and let it change and reflect you each step of your journey. Invite in those you wish to invite; you decide who gets access to your home.

Your own place in the world. No other fort like yours, and it is gorgeous. It's needed. Nothing can bring it down, not if you don't let it. Let it stay up and let it stand. Take care of it, take care of yourself, stay connected and be home in the world. No matter where you go or where you are, you will always be at home inside of yourself.

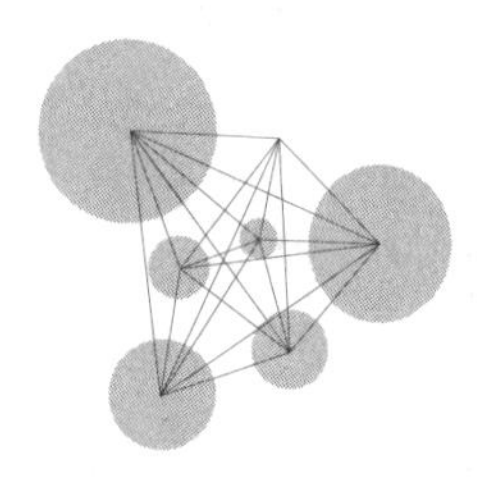

Acknowledgments

To my Father—Thank you for guiding me from above and looking over me as I live more and more. I recognize more and more that you were and still are my greatest teacher. I have learned so much from you, even as I have paved my own path.

To my mother—Thank you for reminding me of all the good I do.

Arielle, Yitzy, Ahron, and Daniel, and by the time this comes out, the new little one ☺— Arielle, you have given me the greatest gift: grandchildren, who are the yummiest, sweetest, kindest gifts I could ever ask for. Watching you become the mother, wife, and human you have grown into inspires me to be a better person and father. Yitzy—thank you for being an awesome son–in–law, and a real thank you for being an amazing husband to my daughter and father to my grandchildren.

Jake—You are a rockstar. Such a hard worker, a lover of my music, a heart of gold, and an inspiration in so many ways. I admire your mind, and I adore your heart—and I adore you with all my heart and soul.

Sarina and Saudia—"Your honesty, transparency, and realness are a true representation of chesed (kindness) in every sense of the word. And Saudia, welcome to the family.

Nate—You are the kindest soul I have ever seen. The way you care about others is remarkable, and I'm so grateful for watching you turn into a real mensch.

Evie—You are and will always be my baby! You are growing up into such a magnificent young lady and I keep on being amazed at your maturity, honesty, and transparency.

To my siblings—Thank you for all being role models for me and so many others.

A special thank you to my sister Malke, who literally reads my thoughts and encourages me, even without me knowing when I need it. You are our leader and take care of all of us.

Abe—Thank you for paving the way and showing up for me.

To my community of addicts, those in and out of recovery, those struggling with mental health challenges, and anyone and everyone who chooses to work on themselves. I get way more out of giving than getting. You show me how to be a better person, and your courage to work on yourselves and show up as you are gives me the courage to show up as I am, letting me take off my mask and come out of the closet called shame.

I am Jewish and take huge pride in being Jewish. Yet, I have to say the 12-step rooms are steeped in the greatest sense of spirituality, where we all come to better ourselves, and no one cares who your parents are, where you have come from, what religion you abide by, what your politics are, or how much money you have—or don't.

To my best friends—You know who you are, and I love you so much. To what I like to call Friends of Asher, you are my rocks. And to my adopted children—I love you.

To Tami—Thank you for being the best mom and my partner.

To Chaiky—Thank you for seeing me and accepting and loving me. Thank you for being who you are to me in my life. There is no greater compliment.

To my therapists, teachers, guides, and rabbis—you have advised spot on (especially when I have taken it). You have shown me how to be a man.

To Katya—You are the best partner I could ever imagine. You are a gifted writer but, more important, a gifted human. Thank you for being part of my inner circle.

Kristen—Without you and your confidence in me, this book would have never become a reality. Thank you for believing in me, encouraging me, and showing me I can do it.

Thank you so much to all those who have read, commented, and supports this book. To my men's group and to my Nexus cohort, who have supported me and pushed me. I adore you guys so much.

And last but not least, thank you, God, my Higher Power, whom I choose to call Hashem. I used to think you were the big bad wolf who would blow my house down if I didn't do what you said. Little did I know you love me just because I'm me. You guide me, care for me, and exude only love. You sometimes kick me into gear out of love and let me fall on my face, as that is sometimes the only way I listen. Yet, when I pay attention, I can see all the beauty you have created and continue to create on a daily basis. Thank you.

P.S.—I still have many questions, which I will probably ask them until this part of the journey is over.

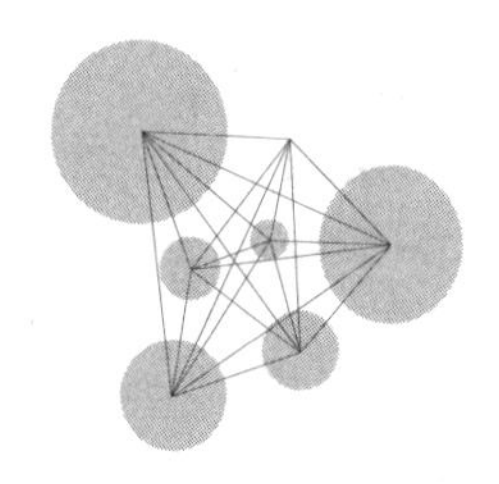

About the Author

Asher is a spiritual entrepreneur, human connection coach and Rabbi in Southern California. His story began at home as a young child where all seemed well from the outside. As the youngest by nine years, he felt a horrible sense of abandonment. His loneliness was compounded by his father's prominence as a rabbi and community leader where the pressure to appear as role models was insufferable. This resulted in a childhood eating disorder and drug use by age 14.

Asher was 33 when he lost his multi–million–dollar business, with the resulting bankruptcy destroying what little self–worth he had as a provider to his family – he had hit rock–bottom. Asher found his road to recovery through the rooms of Alcoholics Anonymous, where despite the circle of anonymous faces, it was truly the first time in his life he felt the power of shared human connection through service to self and others.

The experience marked the debut of an odyssey of self–discovery, trading ego for vulnerability, and leaving the pursuit of pleasure for the pursuit of meaning. Asher decidedly dedicated the rest of his career to helping others help themselves "restore wholeness" in their lives.

Armed with a renewed sense of self, profound life experience, and entrepreneurial passion, Asher founded Transcend in 2008, building an internationally recognized recovery community. Now sober twelve years and counting, Asher has counseled hundreds of men and women and built a renowned reputation where he is recognized by his three hallmark pillars of recovery: *Accountability, Community,* and *Unconditional Love.*